KLASSENARBEITEN ENGLISCH

W0250506

Liam Cleary

Englisch 7. Klasse

mit Audio-CD

für G8

STARK

Bildnachweis:
S. 37: http://commons.wikimedia.org/wiki/Image:AlaskaStateSealTransparent.png
S. 61: CorelDraw Inc
S. 78–79: © David Fuchs, Berlin
S. 94, 134, 150: © Liam Cleary
S. 115: © Duncan Gilbert /www.dreamstime.com
S. 127 Temple Bar: http://de.wikipedia.org/wiki/Bild:TempleBar.jpg
S. 127 Book of Kells, Dublin Tour Bus: © Liam Cleary
S. 157 Guy Fawkes: © Hulton Archive /Getty Images
S. 157 Globe Theatre:
http://commons.wikimedia.org/wiki/Image:Southwark_reconstructed_globe.jpg

ISBN 978-3-86668-010-4

www.stark-verlag.de
1. Auflage 2008

Inhalt

Autor: Liam Cleary

Vorwort

Liebe Schülerin, lieber Schüler,

dieses Buch hilft dir, dich gründlich auf **Tests** und **Klassenarbeiten** im Fach Englisch vorzubereiten. Alle Tests und Klassenarbeiten sind mit **Zeitangaben** zur Orientierung, ausführlichen **Lösungsvorschlägen** und einem **Notenschlüssel** versehen, damit du deine Leistungen selbst kontrollieren kannst. Beim Überprüfen deiner Fortschritte solltest du außerdem die folgenden Hinweise beachten:

- Bei den Diktaten ***(dictation)*** ist immer eine Gesamtpunktzahl angegeben, die du bekommst, wenn du alles richtig hast. Für jeden Fehler ziehst du dir zwei Punkte von dieser Gesamtpunktzahl ab, für Fehler in der Groß- und Kleinschreibung oder in der Getrennt- und Zusammenschreibung nur einen Punkt.
- Auch für Textproduktionen ***(composition)*** gibt es eine Gesamtpunktzahl. Diese verteilt sich zu 1/3 auf den Inhalt und zu 2/3 auf die Sprache. Bei den Punkten für die Sprache ziehst du dir für jeden Fehler einen Punkt ab. Angaben zur Punkteverteilung im inhaltlichen Teil findest du in den Hinweisen zu den Lösungen. Bei einer Aufgabe mit z. B. 21 Punkten, entfallen 14 auf Sprache und 7 auf Inhalt. Hast du z. B. 5 Rechtschreibfehler gemacht, musst du dir im sprachlichen Bereich 5 Punkte abziehen und erhältst 9 Punkte. Hast du im inhaltlichen Bereich z. B. 5 Punkte, dann bekommst du für die Aufgabe insgesamt 14 Punkte.
  Beachte: Bei den Lösungen zu den Aufgaben in diesem Buch handelt es sich immer nur um Lösungsvorschläge. Sie dienen der Orientierung, denn hier gibt es kein einfaches „Richtig" oder „Falsch". Mithilfe der Lösungsvorschläge kannst du aber überprüfen, welche inhaltlichen Elemente in der Lösung enthalten sein müssen und wie ein Text aussehen könnte.
- Bei den Übersetzungsaufgaben ***(translation)*** ist für jeden Satz eine feste Punktzahl vorgegeben. Wenn du den Satz komplett richtig übersetzt hast, bekommst du die volle Punktzahl. Für jeden Fehler ziehst du dir einen Punkt ab.
- Bei Mediationsaufgaben ***(mediation)*** bekommst du die volle Punktzahl, wenn du alle inhaltlichen Aspekte übertragen hast. Für sprachliche Fehler im Englischen oder Deutschen ziehst du dir Punkte ab.
- Bei Aufgaben zum Wortschatz ***(vocabulary)*** oder zur Grammatik ***(grammar)*** ist ebenfalls eine feste Punktzahl vorgegeben. Für Fehler musst du dir entsprechend Punkte abziehen.

Du musst dieses Buch übrigens nicht von Anfang bis Ende durcharbeiten. Du kannst dir auch Aufgaben in den Bereichen heraussuchen, die du besonders üben möchtest.

Viel Erfolg bei der nächsten Klassenarbeit!

Liam Cleary

Kurzgrammatik

1 Adverbien – *adverbs*

Bildung Adjektiv + *-ly*	glad → gladly
Ausnahmen: • *-y* am Wortende wird zu *-i*	easy → easily funny → funnily
• auf einen Konsonanten folgendes *-le* wird zu *-ly*	simple → simply probable → probably
• auf einen Konsonanten folgendes *-ic* wird zu *-ically*	fantastic → fantastically
Ausnahme:	public → publicly
Beachte: • In einigen Fällen haben Adjektiv und Adverb dieselbe Form.	daily, early, fast, hard, long, low, weekly, yearly
• Unregelmäßig gebildet wird:	good → well
• Endet das Adjektiv auf *-ly*, so kannst du kein Adverb bilden und verwendest deshalb: *in a* + Adjektiv + *manner*	friendly → in a friendly manner

Verwendung Adverbien bestimmen • Verben,	She easily found her brother in the crowd. *Sie fand ihren Bruder leicht in der Menge.*
• Adjektive oder	This band is extremely famous. *Diese Band ist sehr berühmt.*
• andere Adverbien näher.	He walks extremely quickly. *Er geht äußerst schnell.*

2 Bedingungssätze – *if-clauses*

Ein Bedingungssatz besteht aus zwei Teilen: Nebensatz (*if*-Satz) + Hauptsatz.
Im ***if*-Satz** steht die **Bedingung**, unter der die im **Hauptsatz** genannte **Folge** eintritt.

Bedingungssatz Typ I

Bildung

- *if*-Satz (Bedingung): Gegenwart *(simple present)*

If you read this book,
Wenn du dieses Buch liest,

- Hauptsatz (Folge): Zukunft mit *will (will-future)*

you will learn a lot about Scotland.
erfährst du eine Menge über Schottland.

Der *if*-Satz kann auch nach dem Hauptsatz stehen:

- Hauptsatz: *will-future*

You will learn a lot about Scotland,
Du erfährst eine Menge über Schottland,

- *if*-Satz: *simple present*

if you read this book.
wenn du dieses Buch liest.

Im Hauptsatz kann statt *will-future* auch

- *can* + Grundform des Verbs oder

If you go to London, you can see Sandy.
Wenn du nach London gehst, kannst du Sandy treffen.

- *must* + Grundform des Verbs

stehen.

If you go to London, you must visit Big Ben.
Wenn du nach London gehst, musst du dir Big Ben ansehen.

Verwendung

Bedingungssätze vom Typ I verwendet man, wenn die **Bedingung erfüllbar** ist. Man gibt an, was unter bestimmten Bedingungen **geschieht, geschehen kann** oder was **geschehen sollte**.

If it's hot, we will go to the beach.
Wenn es heiß ist, gehen wir an den Strand.

If it's hot, we can go to the beach.
Wenn es heiß ist, können wir an den Strand gehen.

If it's hot, we must go to the beach.
Wenn es heiß ist, müssen wir an den Strand gehen.

Bedingungssatz Typ II

Bildung
- *if*-Satz (Bedingung):
  1. Vergangenheit *(simple past)*
- Hauptsatz (Folge): Konditional I (*conditional I = would* + Grundform des Verbs)

If I went to London,
Wenn ich nach London ginge/gehen würde,
I would visit the Tower of London.
würde ich mir den Tower of London ansehen.

Verwendung
Bedingungssätze vom Typ II verwendet man, wenn die **Erfüllung der Bedingung unwahrscheinlich** ist.

3 Fürwörter – *pronouns*

Besitzanzeigende Fürwörter – *possessive pronouns*

Besitzanzeigende Fürwörter *(possessive pronouns)* verwendet man, um zu sagen, **was (zu) jemandem gehört**. Steht ein besitzanzeigendes Fürwort allein, verwendest du eine andere Form, als wenn es bei einem Substantiv steht:

mit Substantiv	ohne Substantiv		
my	*mine*	This is my bike.	– This is mine.
your	*yours*	This is your bike.	– This is yours.
his/her/its	*his/hers/its*	This is her bike.	– This is hers.
our	*ours*	This is our bike.	– This is ours.
your	*yours*	This is your bike.	– This is yours.
their	*theirs*	This is their bike.	– This is theirs.

Rückbezügliche Fürwörter – *reflexive pronouns*

Die rückbezüglichen Fürwörter *(reflexive pronouns)* **beziehen sich auf das Subjekt** des Satzes **zurück**:

myself	I will buy myself a new car.
yourself	You will buy yourself a new car.
himself/herself/itself	He will buy himself a new car.
ourselves	We will buy ourselves a new car.
yourselves	You will buy yourselves a new car.
themselves	They will buy themselves a new car.

4 Grundform – *infinitive*

Die Grundform mit *to* steht nach

- bestimmten Verben, z. B.:

to agree	zustimmen	
to choose	wählen	
to decide	entscheiden	He decided to wait.
to expect	erwarten	*Er beschloss zu warten.*
to forget	vergessen	
to hope	hoffen	
to manage	schaffen	
to offer	anbieten	
to plan	planen	
to promise	versprechen	
to remember	an etw. denken	
to try	versuchen	
to want	wollen	

- bestimmten Substantiven, z. B.:

idea	Idee	It was her idea to go to the museum.
plan	Plan	*Es war ihre Idee ins Museum zu gehen.*

- bestimmten Adjektiven, z. B.:

difficult	schwer, schwierig	It was difficult to follow her. *Es war schwierig, ihr zu folgen.*

easy	leicht
hard	schwer, schwierig

- den Fragewörtern *what, where, which, who, when, why, how.*

We knew where to find her.
Wir wussten, wo wir sie finden würden.

5 Indirekte Rede – *reported speech*

Die indirekte Rede verwendet man, um **wiederzugeben, was ein anderer gesagt** oder **gefragt hat**.

Bildung
Um die indirekte Rede zu bilden, benötigt man ein **Einleitungsverb**. Häufig verwendete Einleitungsverben sind:

to say, to tell, to add, to agree, to think, to ask, to want to know, to answer

In der indirekten Rede verändern sich die **Fürwörter**, in bestimmten Fällen auch die **Zeiten** und die **Orts-** und **Zeitangaben**.

- Veränderung der **Fürwörter**

	direkte Rede	**indirekte Rede**
persönliche Fürwörter:	I, you, we, you	he, she, they
besitzanzeigende Fürwörter:	my, your, our, your	his, her, their
hinweisende Fürwörter:	this, these	that, those

- **Zeiten**

	direkte Rede	**indirekte Rede**
Keine Veränderung, wenn das **Einleitungsverb** in der **Gegenwart**, der **2. Vergangenheit** (Perfekt) oder der **Zukunft** steht:	Jill says, "I love dancing." *Jill sagt: „Ich tanze sehr gerne."*	Jill says (that) she loves dancing. *Jill sagt, sie tanzt sehr gerne.*
Die Zeit der direkten Rede wird in der indirekten Rede **um eine Zeitstufe zurückversetzt**, wenn das **Einleitungsverb** in der **1. Vergangenheit** steht. Die Zeiten verändern sich dann folgendermaßen:	Jill said, "I love dancing." *Jill sagte: „Ich tanze sehr gerne."*	Jill said (that) she loved dancing. *Jill sagte, sie tanze sehr gerne.*

direkte Rede / **indirekte Rede**		
simple present → *simple past*	Joe: “I like it.”	Joe said he liked it.
simple past → *past perfect*	Joe: “I liked it.”	Joe said he had liked it.
present perfect → *past perfect*	Joe: “I’ve liked it.”	Joe said he had liked it.
will-future → *condtional I*	Joe: “I will like it.”	Joe said he would like it.

- Veränderung der Orts- und Zeitangaben:

now	→	then
today	→	that day
yesterday	→	the day before
the day before yesterday	→	two days before
tomorrow	→	the following day
next week	→	the following week
here	→	there

Bildung der indirekten Frage

• Enthält die direkte Frage ein **Fragewort**, **bleibt** dieses in der indirekten Frage **erhalten**. Die **Umschreibung** mit *do/does/did* **entfällt** in der indirekten Frage.	Tom: “When did they arrive?” *Tom: „Wann sind sie angekommen?“*	Tom asked when they had arrived. *Tom fragte, wann sie angekommen seien.*
• Enthält die direkte Frage **kein Fragewort**, wird die indirekte Frage mit ***whether*** oder ***if*** eingeleitet:	Tom: “Are they staying at the youth hostel?” *Tom: „Übernachten sie in der Jugendherberge?“*	Tom asked if/whether they were staying at the youth hostel. *Tom fragte, ob sie in der Jugendherberge übernachten.*

Befehle/Aufforderungen in der indirekten Rede

Häufige Einleitungsverben sind *to tell, to order* (Befehl), *to ask* (Aufforderung).

In der indirekten Rede steht hier **Einleitungsverb + Objekt + *(not) to* + Grundform des Verbs** der direkten Rede.	Tom: “Leave the room.” *Tom: „Verlass den Raum.“*	Tom told me to leave the room. *Tom forderte mich auf, den Raum zu verlassen.*

6 Modale Hilfsverben – *modal auxiliaries*

Im Englischen gibt es zwei Arten von Hilfsverben: die vollständigen Hilfsverben *to be, to have, to do* und die **modalen Hilfsverben** *(modal auxiliaries) can, may, must, shall, will.*

Bildung	
• Die modalen Hilfsverben haben für alle Personen **nur eine Form**, in der 3. Person Singular also kein *-s*.	I, you, he/she/it, we, you, they } must
• Auf das modale Hilfsverb folgt die **Grundform** des Verbs **ohne *to***.	You must listen to my new CD. *Du musst dir meine neue CD anhören.*
• **Frage und Verneinung** werden **nicht** mit *do/does/did* **umschrieben**.	Can you help me? *Kannst du mir helfen?*
Die modalen Hilfsverben können nicht alle Zeiten bilden. Deshalb benötigt man bestimmte **Ersatzformen**.	
• ***can*** (können) *simple past/conditional I: could* Ersatzform: ***to be able to***	I can sing. / I will be able to sing. *Ich kann singen. / Ich werde singen können.*
• ***may*** (dürfen) *conditional: might* Ersatzform: ***to be allowed to***	You may go home early today. / You were allowed to go home early yesterday. *Du darfst heute früh nach Hause gehen. / Du durftest gestern früh nach Hause gehen.*
• ***must*** (müssen) Ersatzform: ***to have to***	He must be home by ten o'clock. / He had to be home by ten o'clock. *Er muss um zehn Uhr zu Hause sein. / Er musste um zehn Uhr zu Hause sein.*
Beachte: *must not/mustn't* = „nicht dürfen"	You must not eat all the cake. *Du darfst nicht den ganzen Kuchen essen.*
„nicht müssen" = *not + to have to*	You don't have to eat all the cake. *Du musst nicht den ganzen Kuchen essen.*

• ***shall*** (sollen) *conditional I: should* Ersatzform: ***to be to, to want***	Shall I help you? / Do you want me to help you? *Soll ich dir helfen?*

7 Partizipien – *participles*

Partizip Präsens – *present participle*

Bildung Grundform des Verbs + *-ing*	read → reading
Beachte: • Stummes *-e* entfällt.	write → writing
• Nach kurzem betontem Vokal wird der Schlusskonsonant verdoppelt.	stop → stopping
• *-ie* wird zu *-y*.	lie → lying

Verwendung Das Partizip Präsens *(present participle)* verwendet man	
• zur Bildung der Verlaufsform der Gegenwart,	Peter is reading. *Peter liest (gerade).*
• zur Bildung der Verlaufsform der Vergangenheit,	Peter was reading when I came into the room. *Peter las (gerade), als ich in den Raum kam.*
• zur Verkürzung eines Nebensatzes oder zur Verbindung von zwei Hauptsätzen mit demselben Subjekt.	

Partizip Perfekt – *past participle*

Bildung Grundform des Verbs + *-ed*	talk → talked

Beachte:	
• Stummes *-e* entfällt.	live → lived
• Nach kurzem betontem Vokal wird der Schlusskonsonant verdoppelt.	stop → stopped
• *-y* wird zu *-ie*.	cry → cried
• Unregelmäßige Verben: siehe Liste. Die *past-participle*-Formen einiger wichtiger unregelmäßiger Verben sind hier angegeben.	be → been have → had give → given go → gone meet → met say → said see → seen take → taken write → written

8 Passiv – *passive voice*

Bildung Form von *to be* + Partizip Perfekt	The Tower Bridge was finished in 1894. *Die Tower Bridge wurde 1894 fertig gestellt.*
Zeitform:	
• *simple present*	Aktiv: Peter buys the milk. Passiv: The milk is bought by Peter.
• *simple past*	Aktiv: Peter bought the milk. Passiv: The milk was bought by Peter.
• *present perfect*	Aktiv: Peter has bought the milk. Passiv: The milk has been bought by Peter.
• *past perfect*	Aktiv: Peter had bought the milk. Passiv: The milk had been bought by Peter.
• *future I*	Aktiv: Peter will buy the milk. Passiv: The milk will be bought by Peter.

- *future II*

Aktiv: Peter will have bought the milk.
Passiv: The milk will have been bought by Peter.

- *conditional I*

Aktiv: Peter would buy the milk.
Passiv: The milk would be bought by Peter.

- *conditional II*

Aktiv: Peter would have bought the milk.
Passiv: The milk would have been bought by Peter.

Aktiv → Passiv

Beachte bei der Umwandlung vom Aktiv ins Passiv:

- Das Subjekt des Aktivsatzes wird zum Objekt des Passivsatzes. Es wird mit *by* angeschlossen.
- Das Objekt des Aktivsatzes wird zum Subjekt des Passivsatzes.

Aktiv: Peter (*Subjekt*) buys the milk. (*Objekt*)
Passiv: The milk (*Subjekt*) is bought by Peter. (*Objekt*)

- Stehen im Aktivsatz zwei Objekte (direktes und indirektes Objekt), lassen sich zwei verschiedene Passivsätze bilden. Eines der Objekte wird zum Subjekt des Passivsatzes, während das zweite Objekt bleibt.

  Beachte:
  Das indirekte Objekt muss im Passivsatz mit *to* angeschlossen werden.

Aktiv: They (*Subjekt*) gave her (*ind. O.*) a ball (*dir. O.*).
Passiv: She (*Subjekt*) was given a ball (*dir. O.*).

oder:

Aktiv: They (*Subjekt*) gave her (*ind. O.*) a ball (*dir. O.*).
Passiv: A ball (*Subjekt*) was given to her (*ind. O.*).

Passiv → Aktiv
Beachte bei der Umwandlung vom Passiv ins Aktiv:

- Das mit *by* angeschlossene Objekt des Passivsatzes wird zum Subjekt des Aktivsatzes; *by* entfällt.
- Das Subjekt des Passivsatzes wird zum Objekt des Aktivsatzes.
- Wenn im Passivsatz der mit *by* angeschlossene Handelnde fehlt, muss im Aktivsatz ein Handelnder als Subjekt ergänzt werden, z. B. durch *somebody, we, you, they.*

Passiv:	The milk	is bought	by Peter.
	Subjekt		*Objekt*
Aktiv:	Peter	buys	the milk.
	Subjekt		*Objekt*

Passiv:	The match	was won.	
	Subjekt		
Aktiv:	They	won	the match.
	(ergänztes) Subjekt		*Objekt*

9 Relativsätze – *relative clauses*

Ein Relativsatz bezieht sich auf eine Person oder Sache des Hauptsatzes und beschreibt diese näher:

The boy who looks like Jane is her brother.
Der Junge, der Jane ähnlich sieht, ist ihr Bruder.

- Hauptsatz: The boy … is her brother
- Relativsatz: who looks like Jane

Bildung
Haupt- und Nebensatz werden durch das Relativpronomen *(who, which, that)* verbunden.

- ***who*** bezieht sich auf **Personen**.

Peter, who lives in London, likes travelling.
Peter, der in London lebt, reist gerne.

- ***which*** bezieht sich auf **Sachen**.

The film "Dark Moon", which we saw yesterday, was far too long.
Der Film „Dark Moon", den wir gestern sahen, war viel zu lang.

- ***that*** bezieht sich auf **Sachen** und auf **Personen** und wird nur verwendet, wenn die **Information** im Relativsatz **notwendig** ist, um den ganzen Satz zu verstehen.

The film that we saw last week was much better.
Der Film, den wir letzte Woche sahen, war viel besser.

Verwendung
Mithilfe von Relativsätzen kannst du **zwei Sätze miteinander verbinden**, wenn sie dasselbe Subjekt haben.

London is England's biggest city. London has about 7.2 million inhabitants.
London ist Englands größte Stadt. London hat etwa 7,2 Millionen Einwohner.

London, which is England's biggest city, has about 7.2 million inhabitants.
London, die größte Stadt Englands, hat etwa 7,2 Millionen Einwohner.

10 Steigerung und Vergleich – *comparisons*

Steigerung des Adjektivs – *comparisons of adjectives*

Bildung
Man unterscheidet

- Grundform — Peter is young.
- 1. Steigerungsform — Jane is younger.
- 2. Steigerungsform — Paul is the youngest.

Steigerung auf *-er, -est*

- einsilbige Adjektive

old, older, oldest
alt, älter, am ältesten

- zweisilbige Adjektive, die auf *-er, -le, -ow* oder *-y* enden

clever, cleverer, cleverest
klug, klüger, am klügsten

simple, simpler, simplest
einfach, einfacher, am einfachsten

narrow, narrower, narrowest
eng, enger, am engsten

funny, funnier, funniest
lustig, lustiger, am lustigsten

Beachte:	
• Stummes *-e* am Wortende entfällt.	simple, simpler, simplest
• Nach einem Konsonanten wird *-y* am Wortende zu *-i-*.	funny, funnier, funniest
• Nach kurzem Vokal wird ein Konsonant am Wortende verdoppelt.	fit, fitter, fittest
Steigerung mit *more …, most …*	
• zweisilbige Adjektive, die nicht auf *-er, -le, -ow* oder *-y* enden	useful, more useful, most useful *nützlich, nützlicher, am nützlichsten*
• Adjektive mit drei und mehr Silben	difficult, more difficult, most difficult *schwierig, schwieriger, am schwierigsten*
Unregelmäßige Steigerung Die unregelmäßig gesteigerten Adjektive solltest du lernen. Einige wichtige Adjektive sind hier angegeben.	good, better, best *gut, besser, am besten* bad, worse, worst *schlecht, schlechter, am schlechtesten* many, more, most *viele, mehr, am meisten* much, more, most *viel, mehr, am meisten* little, less, least *wenig, weniger, am wenigsten*

Vergleich – *sentences with comparisons*

Bildung	
• Wenn du sagen möchtest, dass **zwei Sachen gleich** sind: *as* + Grundform des Adjektivs + *as*	Anne is as tall as John. *Anne ist genauso groß wie John.*
• Wenn du sagen möchtest, dass **zwei Sachen ungleich** sind: *not as* + Grundform des Adjektivs + *as*	John is not as tall as Steve. *John ist nicht so groß wie Steve.*

• Wenn du sagen möchtest, dass **zwei Sachen verschieden** gut/schlecht/ schön ... sind: 1. Steigerungsform des Adjektivs + *than*	Steve is taller than Anne. *Steve ist größer als Anne.*

Steigerung des Adverbs – comparison of adverbs of manner

Adverbien können wie Adjektive auch gesteigert werden.	
• Adverbien auf *-ly* werden mit ***more, most*** bzw. mit ***less, least*** gesteigert.	She talks more quickly than John. *Sie spricht schneller als John.*
• Adverbien, die dieselbe Form wie das Adjektiv haben, werden mit ***-er, -est*** gesteigert.	fast – faster – fastest early – earlier – earliest
• Folgende Adverbien haben unregelmäßige Steigerungsformen:	well – better – best badly – worse – worst

11 Wortstellung – *word order*

Im englischen Aussagesatz gilt die Wortstellung Subjekt – Prädikat – Objekt (*subject – verb – object):*	
• Das Subjekt gibt an, wer oder was etwas tut.	The cat *Die Katze*
• Das Prädikat gibt an, was getan wird.	catches *fängt*
• Das Objekt gibt an, worauf/auf wen sich die Tätigkeit bezieht.	a mouse. *eine Maus.*
Beachte:	
• Orts- und Zeitangaben stehen meist am Satzende.	We will buy a new car tomorrow. *Morgen werden wir ein neues Auto kaufen.* Peter lives in New York. *Peter wohnt in New York.*

- Ortsangaben stehen vor Zeitangaben.

He moved to New York in June.
Er ist im Juni nach New York gezogen.

12 Zeiten – *tenses*

Gegenwart – *simple present*

Bildung
Grundform des Verbs, Ausnahme 3. Person Einzahl: Grundform des Verbs + *-s*

stand – he/she/it stands

Beachte:
- Bei Verben, die auf *-s, -sh, -ch, -x* enden, wird *-es* angefügt.

kiss – he/she/it kisses
rush – he/she/it rushes
teach – he/she/it teaches
fix – he/she/it fixes

- Bei Verben, die auf Konsonant + *-y* enden, wird *-es* angefügt; *-y* wird zu *-i-*.

carry – he/she/it carries

Bildung von Fragen im *simple present*
Umschreibung mit Fragewort + *do/does* + Grundform des Verbs

Where does he live?
Wo lebt er?

Beachte: Die Umschreibung wird nicht verwendet,
- wenn nach dem Subjekt gefragt wird (mit *who, what, which*).

Who came to the party?
Wer kam zur Party?
What happens next?
Was passiert als Nächstes?
Which tree has more leaves?
Welcher Baum hat mehr Blätter?

- wenn die Frage mit *is/are* gebildet wird.

Are you happy?
Bist du glücklich?

Bildung der Verneinung im *simple present*
Umschreibung mit *don't/doesn't* + Grundform des Verbs

He doesn't like football.
Er mag Fußball nicht.

Verwendung
Das *simple present* beschreibt

- Tätigkeiten, die man gewohnheitsmäßig oder häufig ausführt,

  Every morning John buys a newspaper.
  Jeden Morgen kauft sich John eine Zeitung.

- allgemein gültige Aussagen.

  London is a big city.
  London ist eine große Stadt.

Signalwörter: *always, every morning, every afternoon, every day, often, never*

Verlaufsform der Gegenwart – *present progressive*

Bildung
am/is/are + Verb in der *-ing*-Form (Partizip Präsens)

read → am/is/are reading

Bildung von Fragen im *present progressive*
am/is/are + Subjekt + Verb in der *-ing*-Form

Is Peter reading?
Liest Peter gerade?

Bildung der Verneinung im *present progressive*
am not/isn't/aren't + Verb in der *-ing*-Form

Peter isn't reading.
Peter liest gerade nicht.

Verwendung
Mit dem *present progressive* drückt man aus,

- dass etwas **gerade passiert** und **noch nicht abgeschlossen** ist.
  Signalwörter: *at the moment, now*

  At the moment, Peter is drinking a cup of tea.
  Im Augenblick trinkt Peter eine Tasse Tee. [Er hat damit angefangen und noch nicht aufgehört.]

- dass es um eine **zukünftige, bereits festgelegte Handlung** geht.

  We are seeing the match on Sunday.
  Am Sonntag sehen wir uns das Spiel an.

1. Vergangenheit – *simple past*

Bildung Regelmäßige Verben: Grundform des Verbs + *-ed*	walk → walked
Beachte:	
• Stummes *-e* entfällt.	hope → hoped
• Bei Verben, die auf Konsonant + *-y* enden, wird *-y* zu *-i-*.	carry → carried
• Nach kurzem betontem Vokal wird der Schlusskonsonant verdoppelt.	stop → stopped
Unregelmäßige Verben: siehe die Liste in deinem Schulbuch. Die *simple-past*-Formen einiger wichtiger unregelmäßiger Verben sind hier angegeben.	be → was have → had give → gave go → went meet → met say → said see → saw take → took write → wrote
Bildung von Fragen im *simple past* Umschreibung mit Fragewort + *did* + Grundform des Verbs	Why did he look out of the window? *Warum sah er aus dem Fenster?*
Beachte: Die Umschreibung wird nicht verwendet,	
• wenn nach dem Subjekt gefragt wird (mit *who, what, which*).	Who paid the bill? *Wer zahlte die Rechnung?* What happened to your friend? *Was ist mit deinem Freund passiert?* Which boy cooked the meal? *Welcher Junge hat das Essen gekocht?*
• wenn die Frage mit *were* gebildet wird.	Were you happy? *Warst du glücklich?*

Bildung der Verneinung im *simple past* Umschreibung mit *didn't* + Grundform des Verbs	Why didn't you call me? *Warum hast du mich nicht angerufen?*
Verwendung Das *simple past* beschreibt Handlungen und Ereignisse, die **in der Vergangenheit geschehen** und **bereits abgeschlossen** sind. Signalwörter: *yesterday, last week, last year, (five years) ago, in (1999)*	Last week he helped me with my homework. *Letzte Woche half er mir bei meinen Hausaufgaben. [Das Helfen fand in der letzten Woche statt, ist also bereits abgeschlossen.]*

Verlaufsform der 1. Vergangenheit – *past progressive*

Bildung *was/were* + Verb in der *-ing*-Form	watch → was/were watching
Verwendung Das *past progressive* verwendet man, wenn zu einem bestimmten Zeitpunkt in der Vergangenheit eine Handlung abläuft.	Yesterday at 11 o'clock I was still sleeping. *Gestern um 11 Uhr habe ich noch geschlafen.*

2. Vergangenheit – *present perfect simple*

Bildung *have/has* + Partizip Perfekt des Verbs	write → has/have written

Verwendung Das *present perfect simple* verwendet man, wenn	
• ein Vorgang in der Vergangenheit begonnen hat und noch andauert,	He has lived in London since 2002. *Er lebt seit 2002 in London.* *[Er lebt jetzt immer noch in London.]*
• das Ergebnis einer vergangenen Handlung **Auswirkungen auf die Gegenwart** hat.	I have finished my work. *Ich bin mit meiner Arbeit fertig.*
Beachte: *have/has* können zu *'ve/'s* verkürzt werden.	I've eaten your lunch. *Ich habe dein Mittagessen gegessen.* He's given me his umbrella. *Er hat mir seinen Regenschirm gegeben.*
Signalwörter: *already, ever, just, how long, not ... yet, since, for*	
Beachte: Das *present perfect simple* wird oft mit *since* und *for* verwendet (Deutsch: „seit").	
• ***since*** gibt einen **Zeitpunkt** an:	Ron has lived in Sydney since 1997. *Ron lebt seit 1997 in Sydney.*
• ***for*** gibt einen **Zeitraum** an:	Sally has lived in Los Angeles for five years. *Sally lebt seit fünf Jahren in Los Angeles.*

Verlaufsform der 2. Vergangenheit – *present perfect progressive*

Bildung *have/has* + *been* + Partizip Präsens	write → has/have been writing

Verwendung Das *present perfect progressive* verwendet man, um die **Dauer einer Handlung** zu **betonen**, die in der Vergangenheit begonnen hat und noch andauert.	She has been sleeping for ten hours. *Sie schläft seit zehn Stunden.*

Vorvergangenheit – *past perfect*

Bildung *had* + Partizip Perfekt	write → had written
Verwendung Das *past perfect* verwendet man, wenn ein Vorgang in der Vergangenheit vor einem anderen Vorgang in der Vergangenheit abgeschlossen wurde.	He had bought a ticket *Er hatte ein Ticket gekauft,* before he took the train to Manchester. *bevor er den Zug nach Manchester nahm. [Beim Einsteigen war der Kauf abgeschlossen.]*

Verlaufsform der Vorvergangenheit – *past perfect progressive*

Bildung *had* + *been* + Partizip Präsens	write → had been writing
Verwendung Das *past perfect progressive* verwendet man für Handlungen, die in der Vergangenheit bis zu dem Zeitpunkt andauern, zu dem eine neue Handlung einsetzt.	She had been sleeping for ten hours when the doorbell rang. *Sie hatte seit zehn Stunden geschlafen, als es an der Tür klingelte. [Das Schlafen dauerte bis zu dem Zeitpunkt an, als es an der Tür klingelte.]*

Zukunft mit will – *will-future*

Bildung *will* + Grundform des Verbs	buy → will buy
Bildung von Fragen im *will-future* Fragewort + *will* + Grundform des Verbs.	What will you buy? *Was wirst du kaufen?*

Bildung der Verneinung im *will-future*
Fragewort + *won't* + Grundform des Verbs.

Why won't you come to our party?
Warum kommst du nicht zu unserer Party?

Verwendung
Das *will-future* verwendet man, wenn ein Vorgang **in der Zukunft stattfinden** wird.

Signalwörter: *tomorrow, next week, next Monday, next year, in three years, soon*

Beachte: Bei geplanten Handlungen verwendet man das *going-to-future*.

The holidays will start next week.
Nächste Woche beginnen die Ferien.

Zukunft mit going to – *going-to-future*

Bildung
am/is/are + *going to* + Grundform des Verbs

find → am/is/are going to find

Verwendung
Das *going-to-future* verwendet man, um auszudrücken, dass eine **Handlung geplant** ist.

I am going to work in England this summer.
Diesen Sommer werde ich in England arbeiten.

13 Liste unregelmäßiger Verben – *list of irregular verbs*

Infinitiv	**Präteritum**	**Partizip**	**Deutsch**
be	was	been	*sein*
beat	beat	beaten	*schlagen*
become	became	become	*werden*
bend	bent	bent	*beugen*
begin	began	begun	*beginnen*
blow	blew	blown	*blasen*
break	broke	broken	*brechen*
bring	brought	brought	*bringen*
build	built	built	*bauen*
burn	burnt/burned	burnt/burned	*brennen*
buy	bought	bought	*kaufen*
catch	caught	caught	*fangen*
choose	chose	chosen	*wählen*
cling	clung	clung	*sich festhalten*
come	came	come	*kommen*
cut	cut	cut	*schneiden*
do	did	done	*tun*
draw	drew	drawn	*zeichnen*
dream	dreamt/ed	dreamt/ed	*träumen*
drink	drank	drunk	*trinken*
drive	drove	driven	*fahren*
eat	ate	eaten	*essen*
fall	fell	fallen	*fallen*
feed	fed	fed	*füttern*
feel	felt	felt	*fühlen*
fight	fought	fought	*kämpfen*
find	found	found	*finden*
fly	flew	flown	*fliegen*
forget	forgot	forgotten	*vergessen*
forgive	forgave	forgiven	*vergeben*
get	got	got	*bekommen*
give	gave	given	*geben*
go	went	gone	*gehen*
grow	grew	grown	*wachsen*

Infinitiv	**Präteritum**	**Partizip**	**Deutsch**
hang	hung	hung	*hängen*
have	had	had	*haben*
hear	heard	heard	*hören*
hide	hid	hidden	*verstecken*
hit	hit	hit	*schlagen*
hold	held	held	*halten*
keep	kept	kept	*halten*
know	knew	known	*wissen*
learn	learnt/ed	learnt/ed	*lernen*
leave	left	left	*verlassen*
let	let	let	*lassen*
lie	lay	lain	*liegen*
light	lit	lit	*beleuchten*
lose	lost	lost	*verlieren*
make	made	made	*machen*
meet	met	met	*treffen*
pay	paid	paid	*bezahlen*
put	put	put	*stellen/setzen*
read	read	read	*lesen*
ride	rode	ridden	*fahren/reiten*
ring	rang	rung	*läuten/anrufen*
run	ran	run	*rennen*
say	said	said	*sagen*
see	saw	seen	*sehen*
sell	sold	sold	*verkaufen*
send	sent	sent	*schicken*
shake	shook	shaken	*schütteln*
shine	shone	shone	*scheinen*
shoot	shot	shot	*schießen*
show	showed	shown	*zeigen*
shut	shut	shut	*schließen*
sing	sang	sung	*singen*
sink	sank	sunk	*sinken*
sit	sat	sat	*sitzen*
sleep	slept	slept	*schlafen*

Infinitiv	Präteritum	Partizip	Deutsch
smell	smelt	smelt	*riechen*
speak	spoke	spoken	*sprechen*
spell	spelt	spelt	*buchstabieren*
spend	spent	spent	*ausgeben/ verbringen*
spill	spilt/spilled	spilt/spilled	*verschütten*
stand	stood	stood	*stehen*
steal	stole	stolen	*stehlen*
stick	stuck	stuck	*kleben*
swim	swam	swum	*schwimmen*
take	took	taken	*nehmen*
teach	taught	taught	*lehren*
tear	tore	torn	*reißen*
tell	told	told	*erzählen*
think	thought	thought	*denken*
throw	threw	thrown	*werfen*
understand	understood	understood	*verstehen*
wake	woke	woken	*aufwachen*
wear	wore	worn	*tragen*
win	won	won	*gewinnen*
write	wrote	written	*schreiben*

Test 1
Schwerpunkt: *Dictation*

20 minutes

Dictation (24 pts.)

Listen to the text twice and write it down.
Visit to London
(120 words)

Solution

Dictation

Hinweise: *Das Diktat wird zwei Mal vorgelesen. Einmal ganz und beim zweiten Mal in kleineren Abschnitten. Wenn du beim Diktat gut abschneiden willst, solltest du deine Vokabeln sicher beherrschen, denn so fällt es dir leicht, den diktierten Text zu verstehen. In diesem Diktat gibt es wenige schwierige Vokabeln, aber du solltest Wörter wie „capital", „science", „conquered", „armies" und „thieves" in dein Vokabelheft notieren. Für jeden Fehler musst du dir zwei Punkte abziehen.*

Visit to London
London, the capital city of England, has always been a wonderful place for parents and children. When I was there with my family we went to the London Eye, Tower Bridge and visited a science museum. My children loved listening to the guides who told us stories about the Crown Jewels or Henry VIII. Later we met scientists who described many of the scientific discoveries that have been made. We also saw a prince and travelled on the underground. My daughter Patricia is very interested in history so we went to a museum to find out more about the groups of invaders who conquered Britain. We learned about battles, armies, empires, revolutions and thieves as well as groups such as the Anglo-Saxons and the Normans. On television the main stories were about the health service, homelessness and money for the building of new, modern schools. We saw some very good films and we had a really good time!

Notenschlüssel:

1	2	3	4	5	6
24–21	20–18	17–15	14–12	11–9	8–0

Test 2
Schwerpunkte: *Irregular verbs, vocabulary*

20 minutes

I Irregular verbs (10 pts.)

Do you know the three forms of the following verbs? Write them down. You must know all three forms to get one point for each verb.

1.	bauen	build	built	built
2.	wissen	______	______	______
3.	aufwachsen	______	______	______
4.	werden	______	______	______
5.	stehlen	______	______	______
6.	haben	______	______	______
7.	regnen	______	______	______
8.	hören	______	______	______
9.	unterrichten	______	______	______
10.	verlassen	______	______	______
11.	verlieren	______	______	______

II Vocabulary (10 pts.)

Explain what is meant by the following:

1. empty

____

2. (to) invent

____

3. a platform

____

4. (to) reply to someone or something

____

5. scrapbook

____

III Fill in

(10 pts.)

Fill in the missing words in this text.

Many people think that the Queen has a lot ______ money. It is often said that she is one of the ________________ women in the world. However, the Queen also has money problems because she has to ________________ many people who work for her. Although she has ______________ palaces she also has to keep them in good condition. Some years ____________ there was a big fire at Windsor Castle and a lot of ________________ was done. And now a new law says that she has to pay money to the government just like ________________ else. To get more money she has ____________ Buckingham Palace to the public who can now go and see the building. Last summer I ________________ to London and walked through the Palace. It was really beautiful but the ________________ I had to buy to get in was expensive. Just like me the Queen needs money too!

Solution

I Irregular verbs

Hinweise: *Die meisten Verben bei dieser Aufgabe sind unregelmäßig. Wenn du Fehler gemacht hast, wiederhole die unregelmäßigen Verben auf Seite 22–24.*

2.	wissen	know	knew	known
3.	aufwachsen	grow	grew	grown
4.	werden	become	became	become
5.	stehlen	steal	stole	stolen
6.	haben	have	had	had
7.	regnen	rain	rained	rained
8.	hören	hear	heard	heard
9.	unterrichten	teach	taught	taught
10.	verlassen	leave	left	left
11.	verlieren	lose	lost	lost

II Vocabulary

Hinweise: *Hier musst du Wörter erklären. Deine Erklärung soll so genau wie möglich sein. Achte außerdem darauf, dass sie sprachlich gut gestaltet ist.*

1. If a bottle or a box is empty then there is nothing in it. Empty is the opposite of full.
2. To invent something is to create or devise something. James Watt was a great inventor.
3. A platform is a place in a station from where a train departs.
4. To reply to someone or something is to give them an answer.
5. A scrapbook is a book of blank pages into which we stick things such as photos.

III Fill in

Many people think that the Queen has a lot **of** money. It is often said that she is one of the **richest** women in the world. However, the Queen also has money problems because she has to **pay** many people who work for her. Although she has **many** palaces she also has to keep them in good condition. Some years **ago** there was a big fire at Windsor Castle and a lot of **damage** was done. And now a new law says that she has to pay money to the government just like **everyone** else. To get more money she has **opened** Buckingham Palace to the public who can now go and see the building. Last summer I **went** to London and walked through the Palace. It was really beautiful but the **ticket** I had to buy to get in was expensive. Just like me the Queen needs money too!

Notenschlüssel:

1	2	3	4	5	6
30–27	26–23	22–19	18–15	14–11	10–0

Test 3
Schwerpunkte: ***Composition, vocabulary, adjectives***

20 minutes

I Composition
(21 pts.)

Lisa is having trouble with her English homework. She decides to send an e-mail to her English pen-pal Sharon asking her a few questions that are part of her English homework.

These are the questions she asks:

Why is the Globe Theatre famous? For what is Notting Hill well known? When people speak about England, Scotland, Wales and Northern Ireland what phrase do they sometimes use? What's the British flag called? Why is the Prime Minister so important? What's a couch potato?

Write Sharon's short reply of about 50–100 words answering her e-mail and giving her the information she needs.

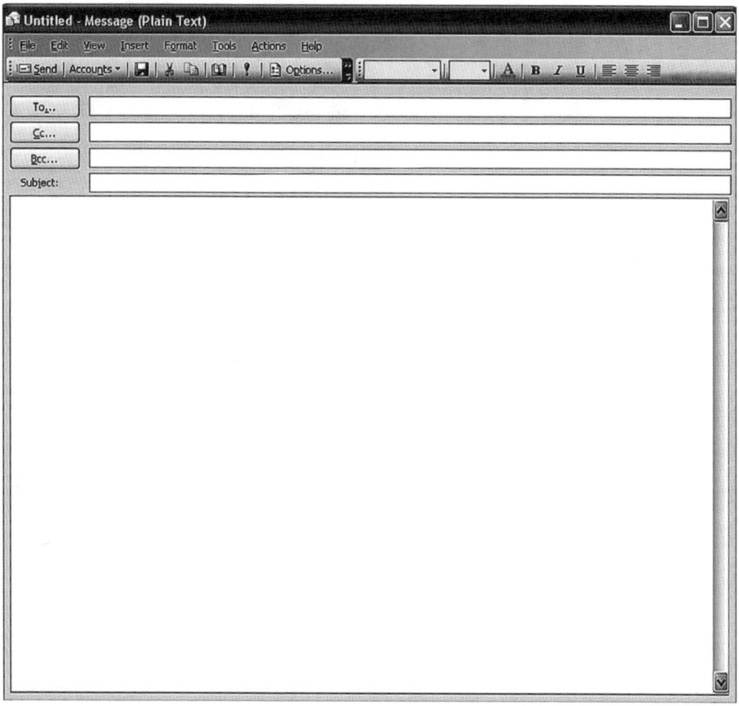

II Vocabulary (8 pts.)

Which word is the odd one out? Explain your choice briefly.

1. meter – color – travelled – flavor: ______________________________

   ____

2. climbing – singing – swimming – running: ____________________

   ____

3. became – taught – drove – wake: ______________________________

   ____

4. television – history – science – maths: ______________________

   ____

III Adjectives (5 pts.)

Find the correct adjectives and fill in the crossword puzzle.

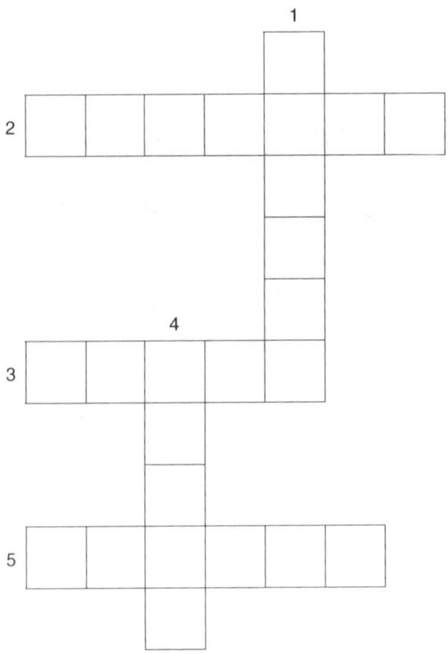

Across

2 A person everybody knows is …

3 This room is untidy, it's really …

5 The book isn't exciting at all, it's …

Down

1 You can't see the sun today, it's too …

4 After the movie I was terrified, it was …

Solution

I Composition

Hinweise: *In den composition Aufgaben musst du selbst kleine Texte schreiben. Hier bekommst du Punkte für die sprachliche Leistung und für den Inhalt. Versuche, einfache Sätze zu schreiben und verwende Vokabeln, bei denen du dir sicher bist, dass sie richtig sind. So vermeidest du unnötige Fehler. Lies dir die Aufgabe genau durch. Du bekommst die volle Punktzahl von 7 für den Inhalt wenn du alle Fragen aus der Aufgabenstellung eingearbeitet hast und die richtige Begrüßung und Verabschiedung gewählt hast. Für jede Frage die du nicht beantwortet hast, musst du dir einen Inhaltspunkt abziehen. Ebenso, wenn du die falsche Begrüßung oder Verabschiedung gewählt hast. Denke daran, dass du eine E-Mail an eine Freundin schreibst.*

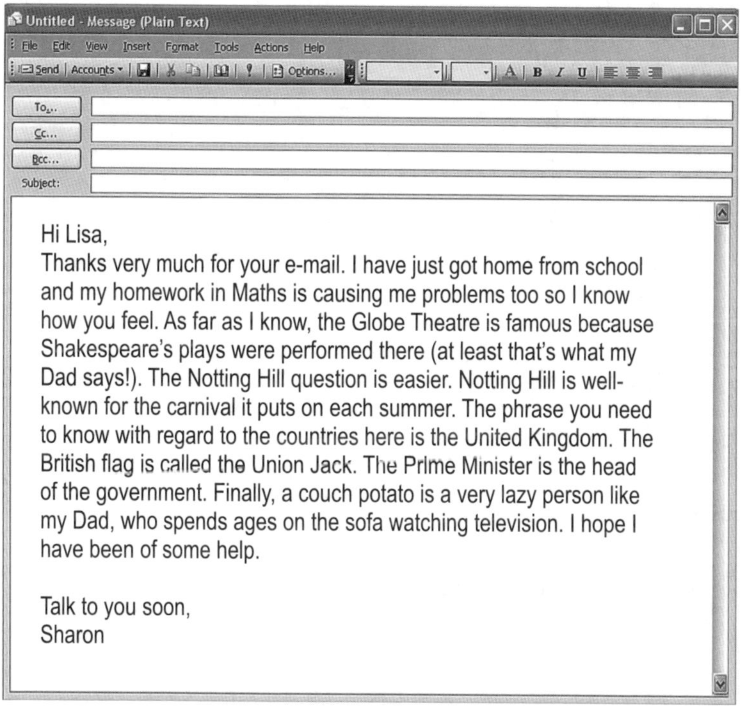

Hi Lisa,
Thanks very much for your e-mail. I have just got home from school and my homework in Maths is causing me problems too so I know how you feel. As far as I know, the Globe Theatre is famous because Shakespeare's plays were performed there (at least that's what my Dad says!). The Notting Hill question is easier. Notting Hill is well-known for the carnival it puts on each summer. The phrase you need to know with regard to the countries here is the United Kingdom. The British flag is called the Union Jack. The Prime Minister is the head of the government. Finally, a couch potato is a very lazy person like my Dad, who spends ages on the sofa watching television. I hope I have been of some help.

Talk to you soon,
Sharon

II Vocabulary

__Hinweise:__ Bei dieser Übung musst du nach Gemeinsamkeiten zwischen den Wörtern suchen und überlegen, welches nicht dazu passt. Die Gemeinsamkeiten können den Inhalt betreffen, aber auch Grammatik und Schreibweise.

1. travelled: it is the only British English word, the others are American.
2. singing: the others are sports.
3. wake: it is the only infinitive, the others are past tense forms.
4. television: the others are school subjects.

III Adjectives

Notenschlüssel:

1	2	3	4	5	6
34–30	29–25	24–21	20–17	16–11	10–0

Test 4
Schwerpunkte: *Tenses, since and for, crossword puzzle*

20 minutes

I Tenses
(17 pts.)

Use the correct form of the verb *(present perfect progressive* or *present perfect simple)* and put in *since* or *for* where necessary.

1. Helen Joyce, who ____________________________ (to wait) for her husband in Main Street in Galway ___________ (since or for) 5 o'clock, is getting very angry. It is now half past seven.
2. John! At last! Where on earth __________________ (you, to be)?
3. Oh! Leave me alone! I have ______________________ (to work) without a break __________________ (since or for) ten and a half hours, without a lunch, without anybody saying please, thank you, or can I help? I'm totally fed up!
4. Well you might ____________________ (to ring) me at least. I do have a mobile you know! I ____________________________ (to stand) here in the cold ______________ (since or for) a long time!
5. I hadn't time. Gosh I'm starving! And thirsty! I hope ______________________ (you, to cook) something nice for tea.
6. Are you mad? Do you think I have nothing else to do? ________________________________ (you, to live) on the moon ______________ (since or for) the day we first met? You know I have a job too!
7. Sorry! I should __________________________ (to know) better. ____________________________ (I, at least, to buy) you some flowers!
8. Oh darling! How thoughtful of you! You remembered it is our wedding anniversary! I bet ___________________________ (you, to think) of me all day!

9. Of course, dear. Come on now, I ________________ (to be) a good husband. Buy me a meal! My stomach ________________ (to have) an empty feeling ___________ (since or for) 5 o'clock!

II Since or for?

(3 pts.)

Change each of these sentences so that you can use *since* instead of *for* or *for* in place of *since*.

1. John Kelly has been living in Boston since 1956.

   ____

2. I have been going to Fountain High School since I was 11.

   ____

3. You know I'm getting a bit worried. Will he be able to play tomorrow? Today is Saturday and he has been ill for three days.

   ____

III Crossword puzzle

(12 pts.)

Find the right words to complete the crossword puzzle.

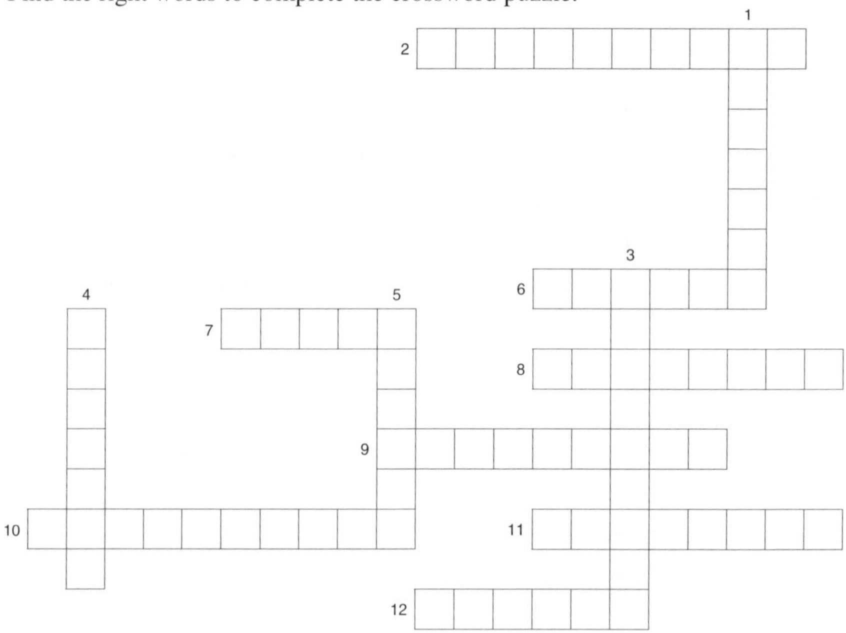

Across
2 The number of people who live in a country or city
6 The opposite of past
7 Something you need to clean your teeth
8 It tells you about the weather for the next few days
9 A place where you can do sports indoors
10 A book where you can look up unknown words
11 You need it when you go on holiday
12 Harry Potter is a famous …

Down
1 What you say when you leave someone
3 If you are very frightened, you are …
4 The British English word for "cookie"
5 I need to eat something, I'm so …

Solution

I Tenses

Hinweis: *Die Regeln zur Bildung und zur Verwendung des „present perfect" und des „present perfect progressive" kannst du in der Kurzgrammatik auf S. 19 nachlesen.*

1. Helen, who **has been waiting for** her boyfriend in Main Street in Galway **since** 5 o'clock, is getting very angry. It is now half past seven.
2. "John! At last! Where on earth **have you been**?"
3. Oh! Leave me alone! I **have worked/have been working** without a break **for** ten and a half hours, without a lunch, without anybody saying please, thank you, or can I help? I'm totally fed up!
4. Well you might **have rung** me at least. I do have a mobile you know! I **have been standing** here in the cold **for** a long time!
5. I hadn't time. Gosh I'm starving! And thirsty! I hope **you have cooked** something nice for tea.
6. Are you mad? Do you think I have nothing else to do? **Have you been living** on the moon **since** the day we first met? You know I have a job too!
7. Sorry! I should **have known**. **I have at least bought** you some flowers!

8. Oh darling! How thoughtful of you! You remembered it is our wedding anniversary! I bet you **have been thinking** of me all day!
9. Of course dear. Come on now, I have been a good husband. Buy me a meal! My stomach **has had** an empty feeling **since** 5 o'clock!

II Since or for?

Hinweis: *Die Regeln zur Verwendung von „since" und „for" kannst du in der Kurzgrammatik auf S. 19 nachlesen.*

1. John Kelly has been living in Boston for over forty years.
2. I have been attending Fountain High School for four years.
3. Today is Saturday and he has been ill since Thursday.

III Crossword puzzle

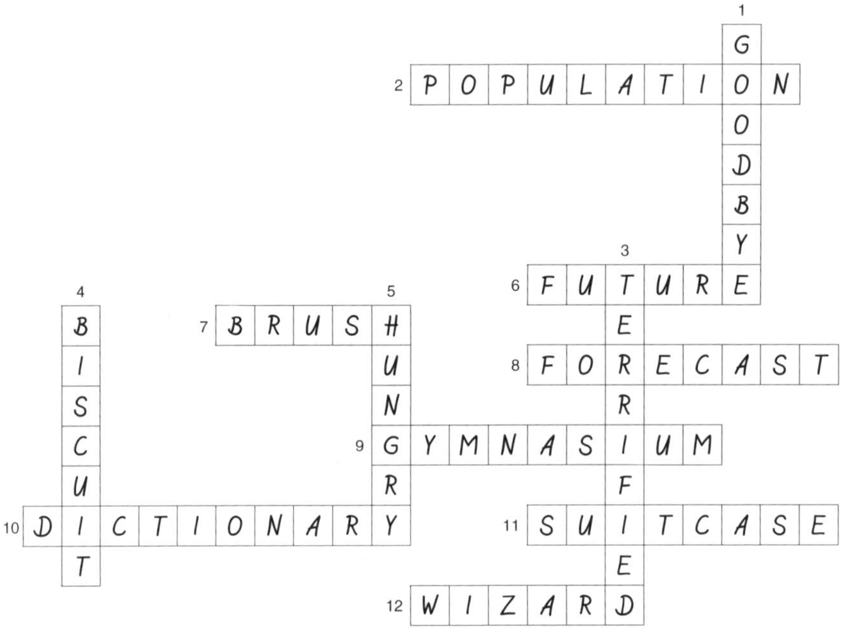

Notenschlüssel:

1	2	3	4	5	6
32–29	28–25	24–21	20–17	16–13	12–0

Test 5
Schwerpunkt: *Listening comprehension*

15 minutes

Listening comprehension

Tracy is showing her exchange student Nick around her home town in Alaska. They start to talk about what life is like in Alaska.

I Mark the correct sentences (12 pts.)

1. Nick and Tracy have known each other all their lives. ☐
2. The name Alaska comes from a word that means great land. ☐
3. Alaska has been part of the USA for many, many centuries. ☐
4. When America bought Alaska from Russia it was not very expensive. ☐
5. The trees on the Alaskan seal stand for all the trees that are planted each year in Alaska. ☐
6. The rays above the mountain represent the Northern Lights. ☐
7. Tracy's Dad is a policeman. ☐
8. Tracy doesn't want to be a policewoman. ☐
9. The town they are in has a lot of crime and murders. ☐
10. It's not that easy to travel around in Alaska. ☐

II Summary (4 pts.)

Look at the following list and choose the right adjectives to describe Alaska or life in Alaska in two or three sentences. Be careful, some adjectives do not fit in:

lonely, beautiful, rainy, icy, snowy, boring, noisy, friendly, mountainous, cut-off, small-minded, historic, wonderful, tired, expensive.

Solution

Hinweis: *Bevor du den Text zum ersten Mal hörst ist es wichtig, dass du dir die Angabe und die Fragen genau durchliest, denn meist findest du hier schon einige Informationen zur Situation, die dich im Text erwartet. Du kannst dann ganz genau auf die Inhalte achten, die du für die Beantwortung der Fragen brauchst. Versuche beim ersten Hören den Gesamtzusammenhang zu verstehen. Wenn du bereits einige Fragen beantworten kannst, mache dir dazu Notizen. Konzentriere dich beim zweiten Hören dann auf die Textstellen, die für die restlichen Fragen wichtig sind. Als Übung kannst du dir den Text auch mehrmals anhören – wenn nötig mit Pausen – und dabei deine Antworten überprüfen. Schwierige Wörter in diesem Text sind: „whaling", „no point in" und „cut off". Lass dich nicht verunsichern, wenn du nicht jedes Wort verstehst, du kannst solche Wörter oft aus dem Zusammenhang erschließen.*

Listening comprehension

Tracy is showing her exchange student Nick around her home town in Alaska. They start to talk about what life is like in Alaska.

TRACY: Well, not everybody knows it but the name "Alaska" comes from a word that meant "great land".

NICK: Well, it's certainly a good name. What's Alaska famous for, Tracy?

TRACY: Alaska is a state famous for its whaling, its cold weather and for Eskimos. In the 19th century, when Alaska first belonged to Russia, many Americans thought only of Alaska as a snowy, icy, cold land which there was no point in buying. Of course, that was before Alaska was discovered by gold seekers, oil companies and tourists. Luckily, President Lincoln was not one of these people and he started talks with Russia that ended with America buying Alaska. It didn't cost very much by modern standards so America got a good bargain when it bought Alaska.

NICK: That's interesting. I see you have the state seal on your Mum's car. What's it made up of?

TRACY: It includes images of icebergs, mining, farming, fisheries, fur seals and a railroad. The rays above the mountains represent the Northern Lights. The train stands for Alaska's railroads and the trees symbolize Alaska's wealth of forests. The fish and the seals show the importance of fishing and wildlife to Alaska's economy.

NICK: That's interesting. Is there anything else I should know about Alaska?

TRACY: Alaska is sometimes called the last frontier and even today there are many places you can only get to by plane. If you are in real trouble your only hope is often to travel by sled with huskies pulling you wherever you want to go.

NICK: Sounds fantastic. Do you like living here?

TRACY: Yes I do. Even though we're a bit cut off from the world, the landscape is wonderful and the people are friendly. It can get lonely at times but there is always something to do.

NICK: What does your Dad do for a living?

TRACY: He's a state policeman. He's been a policeman all his life and loves the job. Even though this is a quiet town there are always jobs for him to do and sometimes he gets me to help him out. I think I'd like to be a policewoman later on.

NICK: Fancy a cup of coffee?

TRACY: Oh yes please. I know a really cute place where they serve great coffee.

NICK: Come on then!

I Mark the correct sentences

1. Nick and Tracy have known each other all their lives. ☐
2. The name Alaska comes from a word that means great land. ☒
3. Alaska has been part of the USA for many, many centuries. ☐
4. When America bought Alaska from Russia it was not very expensive. ☒
5. The trees on the Alaskan seal stand for all the trees that are planted each year in Alaska. ☐
6. The rays above the mountain represent the Northern Lights. ☒
7. Tracy's Dad is a policeman. ☒
8. Tracy doesn't want to be a policewoman. ☐
9. The town they are in has a lot of crime and murders. ☐
10. It's not that easy to travel around in Alaska. ☒

II Summary

Alaska is a bit **cut-off** but it is a **wonderful** place where the landscape is very **beautiful**. It is **snowy** and **icy** there and life can be a bit **lonely** at times but the people are very **friendly**.

Notenschlüssel:

1	2	3	4	5	6
16–14	13–11	10–9	8–7	6–4	3–0

Test 6
Schwerpunkt: *Dictation*

20 minutes

Dictation (20 pts.)

Listen to the text twice and write it down.

From a young girl's diary

(166 words)

Solution

Dictation

Hinweise: *Das Diktat wird zwei Mal vorgelesen. Einmal ganz und beim zweiten Mal in kleineren Abschnitten, sodass du mitschreiben kannst. Die schwierigsten Wörter bei diesem Diktat sind „improve", „terrible" und „horrified". Wenn du diese oder andere Vokabeln falsch geschrieben hast, schreibe sie jetzt in dein Vokabelheft und lerne sie gründlich.*

From a young girl's diary

I had a terrible time at school today. I don't believe I'll never make a good cheerleader. I'm in trouble with my coach, Miss Simpson. When I arrived she said she would kick me off the team if I don't improve. It's so unfair! I want to be a good cheerleader. I love our school but I am useless at sport so cheerleading is my only hope of getting on a team. I have tried everything else from track and field sports to basketball and soccer.

Even the weather is horrible today; grey clouds, showers and a cold wind. Tonight I have to study but at least there's the weekend to look forward to. All the cheerleaders are going for a trip to the park. We're taking packed lunches: Beef sandwiches, sweetcorn and lemonade. My friend Sally loves her new hairstyle. Today, during arts and crafts she spent the whole time looking at herself in the mirror. I would be horrified if I looked like that!

Notenschlüssel:

1	2	3	4	5	6
20–18	17–15	14–12	11–10	9–6	5–0

Test 7
Schwerpunkte: ***Tenses, translation, question on selected topic***

20 minutes

I Mixed bag (12 pts.)

Fill in the gaps. Mainly it's verbs you have to put in but not always. Pay attention to tenses.

Two years ago we __________ (to fly) to Nova Scotia to spend some time with my Uncle Gerard. We ______________________ (never, to be) there before so the whole family ___________ (to be) very excited. Uncle Gerard ______________________ (to emigrate) to Nova Scotia _________ 1967. He ________________ (to speak) with a strong Canadian accent so listening to him was quite strange at first. One day we ________________ (to take) a train to Cape Breton island and I really __________________ (to enjoy) that trip. After a week we _____________________ (to go) off for a week around the whole island and I took _____________ photos _____________ my new camera. At the moment I _______________________ (to sit) in my bedroom looking at them. Next week I ____________________ (to send) Uncle Gerard a selection of the photos for his album.

II Translation (16 pts.)

Translate the following sentences.

1. Mike saß direkt neben mir während des Konzerts. Er freute sich sehr, eine Karte bekommen zu haben.

   ____

   ____

2. Die englische Gruppe Simply Red spielte viele schöne Lieder.

   ____

   ____

3. „Ich habe meine Hausaufgaben überhaupt nicht gemacht“, sagte Mike.

4. „Wen interessiert das?“, erwiderte ich. „Wir haben bis Montag keine Schule.“

III Question on selected topic (2 pts.)

Give an example of how the Normans changed the English countryside and one example of their influence on the English language.

Solution

I Mixed bag

Hinweise: *Die Regeln für die korrekte Verwendung der Zeiten im Englischen findest du in der Kurzgrammatik auf Seite 15–21.*

Two years ago we **flew** to Nova Scotia to spend some time with my Uncle Gerard. We **had never been** there before so the whole family **was** very excited. Uncle Gerard **emigrated** to Nova Scotia **in** 1967. He **speaks** with a strong Canadian accent so listening to him was quite strange at first. One day we **took** a train to Cape Breton island and I really **enjoyed** that trip. After a week we **went** off for a trip around the whole island and I took **many/lots of** photos **with** my new camera. At the moment I **am sitting** in my bedroom looking at them. Next week I **will send** Uncle Gerard a selection of the photos for his album.

II Translation

Hinweise: *Lies zuerst den Text, den du übersetzen sollst, ganz durch. Bei der Übersetzung musst du darauf achten, dass du die Sätze vollständig ins Englische übersetzt. Es ist nicht immer notwendig, jedes einzelne Wort aus dem Text zu übersetzen. Viel wichtiger ist es, dass du angemessene englische Wendungen benutzt. Lies am Ende die deutsche Version sorgfältig und überprüfe den Sinn.*

1. Mike sat right beside me during the concert. He was delighted/very happy/thrilled to have got a ticket.
2. Simply Red, the English pop group, played many nice songs.
3. “I haven’t done my homework at all,” said Mike.
4. “Who cares?” I replied. “We have no/we don’t have school until Monday.”

III Question on selected topic

The Normans built many castles all over England. They helped change the language by bringing many French words into English that weren’t there before.

Notenschlüssel:

1	2	3	4	5	6
30–27	26–23	22–19	18–15	14–11	10–0

Test 8
Schwerpunkte: *Active or passive, plural forms*

15 minutes

I Active or passive? (24 pts.)

Tom Dunne is a guide at Warkworth Castle in England. He is showing some visitors around the castle. He has however forgotten much of what he wanted to say. Fill in the correct *active* or *passive* form of the verbs needed to help him complete the story.

Warkworth Castle ____________________ (to build) in the middle of the 12th century. However, in the 13th century, the owner, Robert FitzRobert, ________________ (to begin) a new castle and the Gatehouse and Tower ___________________ (to finish). Many prisoners __________________ (to keep) in the Tower down through the years and the gatehouse _________________________ (can, to see, still) today. In 1332 the Percys, one of England's strongest and most famous families, ___________________ (to give) the castle by King Edward II. They also _________________ (to own) a huge castle at Alnwick, which _________________________ (later, to become) the location for the *Harry Potter* films. Big improvements ____________ (to make) by the Percys to Warkworth Castle. Even though Alnwick Castle is a much bigger castle the Percys ______________ (to prefer) to live at Warkworth. The Percy family frequently _______________ (to fight) the kings and queens of England and the castle __________ ______________ (to attack, often). However, they _____________ (to keep) the castle until the time of Henry VIII. Around that time the family decided ________________ (to leave) their home. Warkworth Castle __________________ (to take) over by the king. The Percy family later tried to get the castle back but as Catholics they ________________ (to have) a lot of trouble with Queen Elizabeth I. With nobody living in the castle, parts of the building ___________________________________ (to allow, to fall down). Today, tours of the castle __________________ (can, to take) all day and it ________________ (to visit) by thousands of people every year. Many of the main buildings in Warkworth Castle ____________ (to look) well even though they are very old. It ____________ (to be) a lovely place to spend an afternoon. After visiting the castle many people sit down on the grass beside the River Coquet and have lunch!

II Plural forms (10 pts.)

Write down the plural form of these words:

1. volcano ______________________
2. sandwich ______________________
3. news ______________________
4. radio ______________________
5. baby ______________________
6. mouse ______________________
7. leaf ______________________
8. half ______________________
9. foot ______________________
10. army ______________________

Solution

I Active or passive?

***Hinweise:** Die Regeln für die Bildung des Passivs findest du in der Kurzgrammatik auf S. 9–11.*

Warkworth Castle **was built** in the middle of the 12th century. However, in the 13th century, the owner, Robert FitzRobert, **began** a new castle and the Gatehouse and Tower **were finished**. Many prisoners **were kept** in the Tower down through the years and the gatehouse **can still be seen** today. In 1332 the Percys, one of England's strongest and most famous families, **were given** the castle by King Edward II. They also **owned** a huge castle at Alnwick, which **would later become** the location for the *Harry Potter* films. Big improvements **were made** by the Percys to Warkworth Castle. Even though Alnwick Castle is a much bigger castle the Percys **preferred** to live at Warkworth. The Percy family frequently **fought** the kings and queens of England and the castle **was often attacked**. However, they **kept** the castle until the time of Henry VIII. Around that time the family decided **to leave** their home. Warkworth Castle **was taken** over by the king. The Percy family later tried to get the castle back but as Catholics they **had** a lot of trouble with Queen Elizabeth I. With nobody living in the castle, parts of the building **were allowed to fall** down. Today, tours of the castle **can be taken** all day and it **is visited** by thousands of people every year. Many of the main buildings in Warkworth Castle **look** remarkably well even though they are very old. It **is** a lovely place to spend an afternoon. After visiting the castle many people sit down on the grass beside the River Coquet and have lunch!

II Plural forms

1. volcanoes
2. sandwiches
3. news
4. radios
5. babies
6. mice
7. leaves
8. halves
9. feet
10. armies

Notenschlüssel:

1	2	3	4	5	6
34–30	29–25	24–21	20–17	16–11	10–0

Test 9
Schwerpunkte: *If-clauses, opposites*

10 minutes

I If-clauses

(16 pts.)

Fintan and his sister Jenny want to travel to Brighton for a party. Fill in the right words to help them get there.

FINTAN: Wake up Jenny. The sun is rising but if we ____________ (to get up) now, we ____________________ (to arrive) at the train station in time to catch the early train to Brighton.

JENNY: I can't. I can't. I'm just too tired!

FINTAN: I know. You stayed up too late last night.

JENNY: Yes I know that. But if I __________________ (not, to have) a crazy brother then he ________________ (to let) me sleep longer.

FINTAN: Oh leave me alone. If you ______________________ (not, to stop) talking I ______________________ (to throw) a bucket of water on top of you.

JENNY: You wouldn't dare!

FINTAN: Yes I would! And if you __________________ (to go) to bed a bit earlier than you ____________________ (to feel) much fresher every morning.

JENNY: I suppose you're right. If we ________________ (not, to go) now we ____________ never _____________ (to reach) Brighton in time for the party. Come on!

FINTAN: Right you are. And do hurry! Remember if we ___________ (to miss) this train we ____________________ (must, to wait) until 10.30 to catch the next one.

JENNY: Stop talking and move! If you _________________ (to think) less and _______________ (to do) more, life _________________ (to be) so much easier for you!

FINTAN: Very funny! What about breakfast?

JENNY: If we _______________ (to make) the train I ______________ (to treat) you to breakfast on board.

FINTAN: You're on. Let's go!

II Opposites (4 pts.)

Find an opposite for each of these words:

1. (to) lose _________________
2. (to) catch _________________
3. together _________________
4. (to) argue _________________

Solution

I If-clauses

Hinweis: Wenn du bei der Bildung der „If-clauses" noch unsicher bist, schaue dir noch einmal die Regeln dazu in der Kurzgrammatik auf S. 2–3 an.

FINTAN: Wake up Jenny. The sun is rising but if we **get up** now, we **will arrive** at the train station in time to catch the early train to Brighton.

JENNY: I can't. I can't. I'm just too tired!

FINTAN: I know. You stayed up too late last night.

JENNY: Yes I know that. But if I **didn't have** a crazy brother then he **would let** me sleep longer.

FINTAN: Oh leave me alone. If you **don't stop** talking I **will throw** a bucket of water on top of you.

JENNY: You wouldn't dare!

FINTAN: Yes I would! And if you **went** to bed a bit earlier then you **would feel** much fresher every morning.

JENNY: I suppose you're right. If we **don't go** now we **will never reach** Brighton in time for the party. Come on!

FINTAN: Right you are. And do hurry! Remember if we **miss** this train we **will have to wait** until 10.30 to catch the next one.

JENNY: Stop talking and move! If you **thought** less and **did more,** life **would be** so much easier for you!

FINTAN: Very funny! What about breakfast?

JENNY: If we **make** the train I **will treat** you to breakfast on board.

FINTAN: You're on. Let's go!

II Opposites

1. (to) win
2. (to) drop
3. alone, apart
4. (to) agree

Notenschlüssel:

1	2	3	4	5	6
20–17,5	17–15,5	15–12,5	12–10	9–7	6–0

Test 10
Schwerpunkt: *Listening comprehension*

20 minutes

Listening comprehension

Joseph Cain is 24 years old and from New York city. He has decided to try and get some information about his great-great grandfather who came from the town of Bodie in California. Joseph discovers that Bodie is now a ghost town but still decides to go there. He is shown around by Rita McCann, a local tour guide.

I Multiple choice (8 pts.)

Mark the correct answer(s).

1. Joseph's journey was
   - [x] a long, hot one.
   - [ ] one he didn't want to make.
   - [ ] one he had to make for the company he owns.
   - [ ] not one he told his mother about.
2. The town of Bodie is a town
   - [ ] that very few people know about.
   - [ ] that Joseph read about in a book.
   - [x] that many people know about.
   - [ ] that Mrs McCann grew up in.
3. Bodie is
   - [ ] the biggest ghost town in Canada.
   - [ ] the oldest ghost town in America.
   - [ ] the oldest ghost town in California.
   - [x] the biggest ghost town in California.
4. Bodie was
   - [x] a place that was full of gunfighters.
   - [ ] a safe place to live in.
   - [x] a dangerous place to live in.
   - [ ] a town that had no sheriff.

5. The men who worked and lived in Bodie
   - liked to go home at night to their families. [ ]
   - liked to spend their money in shops. [ ]
   - liked to go to saloons and drink. [x]
   - liked to save their money and buy land. [ ]

6. J. S. Cain was Joseph's relation and
   - a teacher in the local school. [ ]
   - a preacher with a family of five. [ ]
   - a man who made a lot of money. [x]
   - a man who was famous throughout the whole town. [x]
   - a man who was poor but hard-working. [ ]

II Questions on the text

1. Explain why the town became a ghost town. (3 pts.)

____

____

____

____

____

2. True or false? Mrs McCann knows what happened to J. S. Cain. Explain your answer. (1 pts.)

____

____

____

Solution

Hinweise: Lies beim Hörverstehen immer zuerst die Aufgaben, sodass du weißt, auf welche Informationen du beim Hören besonders achten musst. Mache dir dabei auch Notizen. Wenn dir das Hörverstehen Probleme bereitet, kannst du als Übung auch Pausen machen oder einzelne Abschnitte mehrmals anhören. Schwierige Vokabeln in diesem Hörverstehenstext sind „dusty", „timber" und „actually".

Listening comprehension

The ghost town of Bodie

Joseph Cain is 24 years old and from New York City. He has decided to try and get some information about his great-great grandfather who came from the town of Bodie in California. Joseph discovers that Bodie is now a ghost town but still decides to go there. He is shown around by Rita McCann, a local tour guide.

JOSEPH: Hello Mrs McCann.

MRS MCCANN: Joseph! Hello, nice to meet you! How was your trip?

JOSEPH: Quite long actually! It got a bit hot but it's good to be here. The town of Bodie is quite difficult to find. I had to drive down that dusty road after turning off state highway 395. Still, it is amazing just how many people know this town. Everybody I asked knew of Bodie and could tell me where it lies.

MRS MCCANN: That is because Bodie is an original ghost town from the late 1800s. A ghost town is a town that was once very rich thanks to the discovery of gold but that has since been deserted. In fact Bodie is the largest ghost town in California and there are still 170 original buildings to be seen.

JOSEPH: Can you tell me a little about the history of the town?

MRS MCCANN: Certainly. In 1859 William Bodey discovered gold here. A mill was built and the town began to grow. It started with about 20 miners and there were almost 8,000 people by 1880! By that time, the town of Bodie was full of families, robbers, miners, store owners and gunfighters of all sorts. It's hard to believe it but there were 60 saloons in town and it wasn't a safe place to live in.

JOSEPH: Did they need that many saloons?

MRS MCCANN: No, but after a hard day's work the miners would head for the bars to spend their money. The mixture of money, gold and alcohol was not good for many men. It's said that there was a man killed every day in Bodie.

JOSEPH: I'm looking for any information you might have about my great-great grandfather. He was known as J. S. Cain.

MRS MCCANN: That's very interesting. Some people got rich in Bodie and not always from mining gold. Your relation, J. S. Cain, owned more buildings and land in Bodie than anyone else. He was quite famous and very rich. He came to Bodie and started shipping timber across the lake. Later he built a bank, as well as many other shops in Bodie.

JOSEPH: So what happened to him?

MRS MCCANN: Well I'm not sure, but once the gold started to disappear the miners left, the shops closed and the people moved away. Bodie's golden days were over. The end came very quickly for Bodie. The rich mines had no more gold and mining companies were losing money. Bodie became a ghost town and it was made into a State Historic Park in 1962. Today, even with less than 10 % of the town still standing, it is the largest ghost town in the western United States. It looks much the same as it did over 60 years ago. But I'll see what I can find out about your great-great grandfather. Maybe he moved back east.

JOSEPH: Thank you very much. That would be great. I'd love to know where he went. Bye-bye!

I Multiple choice

1. Joseph's journey was
   - a long, hot one. ☒
   - one he didn't want to make. ☐
   - one he had to make for the company he owns. ☐
   - was not one he told his mother about. ☐
2. The town of Bodie is a town
   - that very few people know about. ☐
   - that Joseph read about in a book. ☐
   - that many people know about. ☒
   - that Mrs McCann grew up in. ☐
3. Bodie is
   - the biggest ghost town in Canada. ☐
   - the oldest ghost town in America. ☐
   - the oldest ghost town in California. ☐
   - the biggest ghost town in California. ☒

4. Bodie was

   a place that was full of gunfighters. ☒

   a safe place to live in. ☐

   a dangerous place to live in. ☒

   a town that had no sheriff. ☐

5. The men who worked and lived in Bodie

   liked to go home at night to their families. ☐

   liked to spend their money in shops. ☐

   liked to go to saloons and drink. ☒

   liked to save their money and buy land. ☐

6. J. S. Cain was Joseph's relation and

   a teacher in the local school. ☐

   a preacher with a family of five. ☐

   a man who made a lot of money. ☒

   a man who was famous throughout the whole town. ☒

   a man who was poor but hard-working. ☐

II Questions on the text

1. Bodie turned into a ghost town because the gold disappeared, the miners left and the companies shut down. People came to search for gold and when there was no more gold the town died. Soon after the shops, banks and other places shut down and everybody went away.
2. False. She knows a lot about him but not where he went afterwards. She will, however, try and find out.

Notenschlüssel:

1	2	3	4	5	6
12–11	10–9	8–7	6–5	4–3	2–0

Test 11
Schwerpunkte: *Reflexive pronouns, American and British English*

10 minutes

I Reflexive pronouns (11 pts.)

Margo Clarke has a pen-friend, Kerstin Kelly, in Orlando, Florida who she has visited on a number of occasions. Now she is off to see her again. Her parents have taken her to Heathrow Airport and are saying goodbye. Can you fill in the gaps in their conversation by including the missing *reflexive pronouns*?

1. "You mind ________________," her mother said, giving Margo a squeeze. "Of course I will!" she replied.
2. "Don't be worried about me! You two enjoy ________________ while I am in America. Take care of my brother and be happy you have only one child to mind for a while!"
3. "When the Kellys collect you in Orlando be sure and give them the present. It's a nice cake for them and tell them that I baked it ____________________!" said Margo's Dad with a smile on his face.
4. "Oh Dad you couldn't bake a cake even if I paid you!" Margo laughed. "I wouldn't make a fool of ________________ and give them a cake you baked!"
5. "And tell Mr Kelly to get better soon. I heard he hurt __________ playing football."
6. "Yes, he did," Margo said, "but the Kellys have bought ________ a wonderful new car so I suppose he'll be in good form. He loves cars!"
7. "Can I ask if you packed this suitcase ______________________ Margo?" the lady at check-in asked a few minutes later. "Yes we packed it ________________," Margo's mother answered before Margo could say anything.

8. When Margo's parents got back from the airport they made ____________________ a nice cup of tea. "We shouldn't be worrying ____________________," Margo's mother said. "She's a good girl."

9. By that time Margo was already enjoying ____________________, talking to the nice young boy in the seat beside her.

II American and British English (9 pts.)

This table has only been half-completed. Can you finish it?

	British English	**American English**
Different words	autumn	
		apartment
	holiday	
	rubbish	
	trousers	
		candy
Different spelling		center
	programme	
	travelled	

Solution

I Reflexive pronouns

1. "You mind **yourself**," her mother said, giving Margo a squeeze. "Of course I will!" she replied.
2. "Don't be worried about me! You two enjoy **yourselves** while I am in America. Take care of my brother and be happy you have only one child to mind for a while!"
3. "When the Kellys collect you in Orlando be sure and give them the present. It's a nice cake for them and tell them that I baked it **myself**!" said Margo's Dad with a smile on his face.

4. “Oh Dad! You couldn’t bake a cake even if I paid you!” Margo laughed. “I wouldn’t make a fool of **myself** and give them a cake you baked!”
5. “And tell Mr Kelly to get better soon. I heard he hurt **himself** playing football.”
6. “Yes, he did,” Margo said, “but the Kellys have bought **themselves** a wonderful new car so I suppose he’ll be in good form. He loves cars!”
7. “Can I ask if you packed this suitcase **yourself**, Margo?” the lady at check-in enquired a few minutes later. “Yes we packed it **ourselves**,” Margo’s mother answered before Margo could say anything.
8. When Margo’s parents got back from the airport they made **themselves** a nice cup of tea. “We shouldn’t be worrying **ourselves**,” Margo’s mother said. “She’s a good girl.”
9. By that time Margo was already enjoying **herself**, talking to the nice young boy in the seat beside her.

II American and British English

	British English	**American English**
Different words	autumn	*fall*
	flat	apartment
	holiday	*vacation*
	rubbish	*garbage*
	trousers	*pants*
	sweets	candy
Different spelling	*centre*	center
	programme	*program*
	travelled	*traveled*

Notenschlüssel:

1	2	3	4	5	6
20–18	17–15	14–12	11–10	9–8	7–0

Test 12
Schwerpunkte: *Irregular verbs, vocabulary, translation*

20 minutes

I Irregular verbs (13 pts.)

Do you know the three forms of the following verbs? Write them down. You must know all forms to get one point per verb. There are two extra points if you get all the answers right.

1. zeigen ____________ ____________ ____________
2. schließen ____________ ____________ ____________
3. singen ____________ ____________ ____________
4. sinken ____________ ____________ ____________
5. sitzen ____________ ____________ ____________
6. schlafen ____________ ____________ ____________
7. riechen ____________ ____________ ____________
8. buchstabieren ____________ ____________ ____________
9. stehen ____________ ____________ ____________
10. fliegen ____________ ____________ ____________
11. kleben ____________ ____________ ____________

II Vocabulary (6 pts.)

Explain what is meant by the following.

1. beefeater ____
2. familiar ____
3. (to) tremble ____

III Translation (21 pts.)

1. Bis Januar diesen Jahres arbeitete James Deed in einem Krankenhaus in Paris.

   ____

   ____

2. Letzten November wurde eine Frau eingeliefert, die er sehr gut kannte.

   ____

   ____

3. Sie war in der Schule, wo sie als Lehrerin tätig war, zusammengebrochen.

____

____

4. Eine Ärztin untersuchte sie und sagte, dass sie sehr krank sei.

____

____

5. Es war ein Notfall und James musste bei der Operation helfen.

____

____

6. James war wütend, weil es zwei Tage dauerte, die Operation durchzuführen.

____

____

7. Nach der Operation musste die Frau drei Wochen im Krankenhaus verbringen.

____

____

Solution

I Irregular verbs

Hinweise: *Die meisten Verben bei dieser Aufgabe sind unregelmäßig. Falls du Probleme hattest, solltest du die Seiten 22–24 der Kurzgrammatik lernen.*

1.	zeigen	show	showed	shown
2.	schließen	shut	shut	shut
3.	singen	sing	sang	sung
4.	sinken	sink	sank	sunk
5.	sitzen	sit	sat	sat
6.	schlafen	sleep	slept	slept
7.	riechen	smell	smelt	smelt
8.	buchstabieren	spell	spelt	spelt

9. stehen	stand	stood	stood
10. fliegen	fly	flew	flown
11. kleben	stick	stuck	stuck

II Vocabulary

1. A beefeater is a man who guards the Tower of London.
2. If something is familiar we know it and it is not strange to us.
3. To tremble is to shake. Mike started to tremble because he was very nervous about the test.

III Translation

Hinweise: *Lies zunächst den Text sorgfältig. Wenn du deine Übersetzung fertig gestellt hast, lies auch deinen deutschen Text noch einmal und überprüfe den Sinn. Denke daran, nichts auszulassen. Schwierige Vokabeln bei dieser Übersetzung sind „zusammengebrochen: collapsed", „musste: had to" und „wütend: furious".*

1. James Deed worked in a hospital in Paris until January this year.
2. Last November a woman was brought in who he knew very well.
3. She had collapsed in the school where she was working as a teacher.
4. A doctor examined her and said that she was very ill.
5. It was an emergency and James had to help with the operation.
6. James was very angry because it took two days to carry out the operation.
7. After the operation the woman had to spend three weeks in hospital.

Notenschlüssel:

1	2	3	4	5	6
40–36	35–31	30–26	25–20	19–15	14–0

Test 13
Schwerpunkte: *Reported speech, definitions, questions*

15 minutes

I Reported speech (16 pts.)

Read these speech bubbles and then report what the journalist asked Arnold Schwarzenegger. Start like this: *The journalist asked …*

II Definitions

(8 pts.)

Explain what is meant by the following words.

1. audience ______________________________
2. (to) embarrass s.o. ______________________________
3. purse ______________________________
4. pavement ______________________________

III Questions

(6pts.)

Read these answers. Then write a question for the underlined part of the answer.

1. I read my new Dan Brown book <u>last night</u>.

   ____

2. John went <u>to Cork</u> on his holidays last year.

   ____

3. <u>Our new postman</u> spoke to me today.

   ____

Solution

I Reported speech

Hinweise: *Die Regeln zur indirekten Rede findest du auf den Seiten 5–6 der Kurzgrammatik.*

The journalist asked …

… what it was like to live in Hollywood.

… how his first day in America had been.

… if he had thought he would become a film star.

… if his family had been happy he had gone to America.

… how long he had been a politician.

… if he had ever visited the White House.

… what his next film would be called.

… if he travelled a lot.

… if he had gone jogging the day before.

II Definitions

1. An audience is made up of people who come to listen to someone speak, to watch a show or a film, or to enjoy a play.
2. If you embarrass someone you do or say something to make them feel very uncomfortable.
3. A woman keeps her money in a purse.
4. The pavement is at the side of the road and is a place where people can walk.

III Questions

1. When did you read your new Dan Brown book?
2. Where did John go on his holidays last year?
3. Who spoke to you today?

Notenschlüssel:

1	2	3	4	5	6
30–26	25–21	20–18	17–15	14–10	9–0

Test 14
Schwerpunkte: *Listening comprehension*

15 minutes

Listening comprehenion

Dai Jones from Cardiff is on holiday in Queensland. Today he is at the beach and is talking to his friend Aisling Ryan from Brisbane. Aisling doesn't know very much about Wales so she is asking him a few questions.

I Multiple choice (5 pts.)

Mark the correct answer.

1. Dai Jones is
   - working in Queensland for the summer. ☐
   - living in the city of Brisbane. ☐
   - staying in Brisbane to do his exams. ☐
   - on holiday for the summer in Brisbane. ☐
   - visiting his grandfather in Brisbane. ☐
2. Carn Goch is
   - a huge standing stone in Wales. ☐
   - a hill fort in Wales. ☐
   - an example of prehistoric Welsh art. ☐
   - the name of a Welsh coal mine. ☐
3. All the early writings about King Arthur were written
   - only in Welsh. ☐
   - in Welsh or in Latin. ☐
   - only in Latin. ☐
   - in English. ☐
4. Dai plays these sports at school:
   - cricket. ☐
   - rugby. ☐
   - hockey. ☐
   - tennis. ☐

5. Today you can find old Roman roads
   - by flying over Wales in a helicopter. ☐
   - by asking a Welshman to take you to one. ☐
   - in the town of Swansea. ☐
   - by looking at a map. ☐

II True or false?

(7 pts.)

Are these statements true or false? If they are false say why.

	true	false
1. Coal mining is very important in Wales today.	☐	☐
______________________________________		
2. The Holy Grail is somewhere in Wales.	☐	☐
______________________________________		
3. Dai thinks that girls should play rugby.	☐	☐
______________________________________		
4. A seaside holiday in Queensland and in Cardiff are quite similar.	☐	☐
______________________________________		

Solution

Listening comprehension

***Hinweis:** Bitte nicht vergessen: Schwierige Wörter kannst du oft aus dem Zusammenhang erschließen. Meist musst du gar nicht jedes Wort verstehen, um die Fragen zu beantworten. Schwierige Vokablen sind hier „widely-spoken“, „oval“, „shame“.*

Word about Wales

Dai Jones from Cardiff is on holiday in Queensland. Today he is at the beach and is talking to his friend Aisling Ryan from Brisbane. Aisling doesn't know very much about Wales so she is asking him a few questions.

DAI: Queensland is lovely Aisling. I could spend time on a beach like this every day. Our beaches are cold, windy and not exactly the kind of place for a nice holiday.

AISLING: Tell me Dai, what kind of country is Wales?

DAI: Wales is a country with a long history. There are many prehistoric sites, standing stones and hilltop forts in Wales. Carn Goch, near Llangadog, is one of the largest forts. That's a Welsh name. Many people speak Welsh though you will hear a lot of English as well. Welsh is the most widely-spoken of all the Celtic languages to be found in Britain.

AISLING: Weren't the Romans in Wales?

DAI: Yes they were. Today you can still follow in the footsteps of the Roman soldiers who spent time in Wales. They were great road builders. They built roads and joined their forts and camps throughout Wales and even today it's easy to find them with a good map. Some of these old roads are now part of the modern road network.

AISLING: So name me a famous Welsh person – I've never heard of any!

DAI: What? Are you mad! Never heard of Tom Jones the singer? And Catherine Zeta Jones! King Arthur is also part of Welsh history. In fact all the earliest writings that refer to him were written in Welsh or in Latin by Welsh monks. My grandfather says the castle above Llangollen is the hiding place for the Holy Grail.

AISLING: So what industries do you have?

DAI: For many years Wales was a country where coal mining was a very important industry but that has changed as most of the coal mines were closed down some years ago. My cousins all worked in the mines. Now farming and car-making are very important as well as tourism.

AISLING: What sports do you play at school?

DAI: I'm a rugby player. Wales has always had many great rugby players.

AISLING: Oh I know that! Rugby is that funny sport played with an oval ball. We have that here too. So show me how to play it then.

DAI: What! Don't be silly. You can't play rugby!

AISLING: Why not?

DAI: You're a girl, you're not strong enough and it would be a shame to hurt you! Girls and rugby just don't go together.

I Multiple choice

1. Dai Jones is

working in Queensland for the summer.	☐
living in the city of Brisbane.	☐
staying in Brisbane to do his exams.	☐
on holiday for the summer in Brisbane.	☒
visiting his grandfather in Brisbane.	☐

2. Carn Goch is
   - a huge standing stone in Wales. ☐
   - a hill fort in Wales. ☒
   - an example of prehistoric Welsh art. ☐
   - the name of a Welsh coal mine. ☐

3. All the early writings about King Arthur were written
   - only in Welsh. ☐
   - in Welsh or in Latin. ☒
   - only in Latin. ☐
   - in English. ☐

4. Dai plays these sports at school:
   - cricket ☐
   - rugby ☒
   - hockey ☐
   - tennis ☐

5. Today you can find old Roman roads
   - by flying over Wales in a helicopter. ☐
   - by asking a Welshman to take you to one. ☐
   - in the town of Swansea. ☐
   - by looking at a map. ☒

II True or false?

	true	false
1. Coal mining is very important in Wales today. Coal mining is not as important as it used to be.	☐	☒
2. The Holy Grail is somewhere in Wales.	☒	☐
3. Dai thinks that girls should play rugby. He thinks girls are not strong enough to play rugby and would only get hurt.	☐	☒
4. A seaside holiday in Queensland and in Cardiff are quite similar. Welsh beaches are windy and cold whereas the ones in Queensland are warm and sunny and just right for a holiday.	☐	☒

Notenschlüssel:

1	2	3	4	5	6
12–11	10–9	8–7	6–5	4–3	2–0

Test 15
Schwerpunkt: *Mediation, modal verbs*

20 minutes

I Mediation: Rules in the classroom (22 pts.)

The following rules are on a poster in your classroom but the American exchange student who is in your class for three weeks doesn't understand them. Please explain in English.

- Alle Schüler müssen pünktlich zu Stundenbeginn im Klassenzimmer sein.
- Alle Bücher und Hefte müssen mitgebracht werden. Zwei Schüler dürfen sich ein Englischbuch teilen.
- Wer die Hausaufgabe vergessen hat, muss dem Lehrer dies zu Beginn des Unterrichts mitteilen. Der Lehrer kann eine zusätzliche Hausaufgabe aufgeben, falls jemand die Hausaufgabe zu oft vergisst.
- Alle behandeln sich höflich. Wenn jemand spricht, darf niemand unterbrechen.

II Fill in (12 pts.)

1. One year ago Jackie's family moved back to England and she ________________ *(müssen)* to change schools.
2. She and her mother ________________ *(suchen)* for a while until at last they ________________ *(finden)* a new secondary school for her to go to.
3. But she ________________ *(nicht dürfen)* wear normal clothes at school.
4. She ________________ *(müssen)* to wear a uniform.
5. Jackie ________________ *(sein)* very disappointed.
6. "I don't know if I ________________ *(können)* do that," she told her mother with tears in her eyes.
7. "You ________________ *(nicht brauchen)* be worried," her mother replied.

8. “I ____________________________ *(tragen, müssen)* a uniform too when I was your age.”

9. “When you come home for the holidays you _________________ ____________________ *(werden, tragen, können)* all your normal skirts and blouses.”

10. When her mother said that Jackie laughed and it was clear she ______________ *(sich fühlen)* a lot better.

Solution

I Mediation: Rules in the classroom

Hinweis: *Für diese Mediation musst du die „modal auxiliaries" gut beherrschen. Falls du hier Probleme hast, solltest du S. 7 in der Kurzgrammatik noch einmal anschauen. Da es sich hier um eine Mediation handelt, musst du nicht jedes Wort übersetzen, du musst aber darauf achten, dass alle wichtigen Informationen übertragen werden.*

All the pupils have to be in the classroom before the lesson begins. You must bring along all your books and exercise books. For the English lesson we are allowed to share a book with the person sitting beside you. If you have forgotten your homework, you have to tell the teacher before the lesson starts. The teacher can give you extra homework if you forget your homework too often. Everybody has to be polite. When someone is speaking nobody is allowed to interrupt.

II Fill in

1. One year ago Jackie's family moved back to England and she **had to** change schools.
2. She and her mother **searched** for a while until at last they **found** a new secondary school for her to go to.
3. But she **could not** wear normal clothes at school.
4. She **had to** wear a uniform.
5. Jackie **was** very disappointed.
6. "I don't know if I **can** do that," she told her mother with tears in her eyes.
7. "You **needn't** be worried," her mother replied.
8. "I **had to wear** a uniform too when I was your age."
9. "When you come home for the holidays you **will be able to wear** all your normal skirts and blouses."
10. When her mother said that Jackie laughed and it was clear she **felt** a lot better.

Notenschlüssel:

1	2	3	4	5	6
34–31	30–27	26–23	22–17	16–12	11–0

Test 16
Schwerpunkte: *Composition*

20 minutes

Composition (24 pts.)

You are on a visit to your cousin Gareth, in Swansea, Wales. Today is Friday and you are writing an e-mail to your American pen-friend Jim.
Describe:

- what you have done so far,
- which places and activities you liked best and why,
- what your plans are for tomorrow.

Ask Jim some questions about Boston, the city where he lives e. g. weather, school holidays, things to do.
Write about 150 words.

Solution

Composition

***Hinweise:** Bei dieser Textproduktion erhältst du maximal 8 Punkte auf Inhalt und 16 auf Sprache.*

Dear Jim,

How are you? Thanks for your e-mail. I'm writing from Swansea. I have been here since last week. So far I have visited two museums and a Rugby stadium. Yesterday we went cycling to a nearby town. I have gone swimming twice. Tomorrow is going to be super. We have tickets to see a pop concert that Pink is giving in Cardiff. Afterwards we want to go for a meal. Gareth is a big football fan and he loves Cardiff City! How are things in Boston? What's the weather like? How long will you have holidays for? Write soon!

Yours sincerely,

Tom

Notenschlüssel:

1	2	3	4	5	6
24–21	20–18	17–15	14–12	11–9	8–0

Test 17
Schwerpunkt: *Reading comprehension*

20 minutes

Reading comprehension

A short history of smuggling[1]

Smuggling is not something new. It goes back to the year 1275 when men called 'owlers' smuggled wool out of England. They were called 'owlers' because of the noise they made when sending each other messages. Edward I was the king of England at that time and he had placed a tax[2] on wool, which was badly needed in Europe. Ever since smuggling started governments have tried to stop smugglers by using customs officers[3] to search people entering or leaving the country. In 1661 smuggling wool to other European countries was made illegal and smugglers could be killed for this crime. Smugglers soon began using weapons[4] and they often had to fight the British Army. Smugglers were sometimes very violent men but many were only trying to earn money or have things such as whiskey or tobacco that they could not normally buy. In the 18th century men began to smuggle all sorts of goods such as watches, tea and other valuable goods. Smugglers used fast ships and it was very hard to stop or catch them. Smugglers often hid their goods in the sea for many months until it was safe to bring them to towns and villages. Smugglers knew the coast very well and could usually choose from one of many caves to hide in. After a while a new type of smuggling grew up. Men began to make their own whiskey and sell it to their neighbours. This whiskey was often dangerous to drink and not as good as the whiskey made in factories. If the police found a whiskey still, which was where the illegal whiskey was made, they took it away and destroyed it. In Scotland nearly all farmers made their own whiskey and it took many years to stop people doing this. Most people liked smugglers. One famous writer said that a smuggler is a person who would normally be a good man if the country he lived in was not so bad. Tom Johnston is a good example of a well-liked smuggler. He was one of the most famous smugglers ever. By the age of 12 he knew the south coast of England well enough to act as a pilot and by 15 he was a smuggler himself. It was said that women, children, dogs and horses loved him. His life is a story of money, time in prison, injuries and smuggling. He worked for both the French and English governments when they were fighting each other and became very rich.

As time passed the government gave officers more power to try and catch these smugglers. By the 20th century the customs officers had got better at doing this and many smugglers ended up in prison. Today there is still a lot of smuggling going on. Whiskey and cigarettes are still smuggled in but it is drugs that make smugglers very rich.

Annotations
1 *(to) smuggle*: schmuggeln
2 *tax:* Steuer
3 *customs officer:* Zollbeamter
4 *weapons:* Waffen

I True or false? (10 pts.)

Say if the following sentences are true or false. Write down the correct sentence.

	true	false
1. All the smugglers were bad, violent men who were very dangerous and had often spent time in prison.	☐	☐
2. The first smugglers were called 'owlers'.	☐	☐
3. It was fairly easy for the army to catch smugglers.	☐	☐
4. Edward I caused the first smuggling to happen when he put tax on wool.	☐	☐
5. Many people hated smugglers and told the army about them.	☐	☐
6. Smuggling stopped in the 20th century.	☐	☐
7. Smugglers were well able to hide the goods they smuggled.	☐	☐

II Questions on the text (6 pts.)

1. Tom Johnston was a typical smuggler. What, according to the text, was it that made him so typical of the kind of smugglers who lived around his time?

____

____

____

2. Why was the making of illegal whiskey a problem?

____

____

____

Solution

***Hinweise:** Lies den Text zunächst ein Mal durch und versuche zu verstehen, worum es insgesamt geht. Lies dann die Fragen und suche nach den Textstellen, in denen du Informationen dazu findest. Du kannst diese z. B. bunt markieren. Wie beim Hörverstehen können auch in Lesetexten Wörter auftauchen, die du noch nicht kennst, die du aber meist aus dem Zusammenhang erschließen kannst. Oft ist es für die Beantwortung der Fragen auch gar nicht notwendig, jedes einzelne Wort zu verstehen. Gib immer eine Antwort, auch wenn du dir nicht ganz sicher sein solltest, sonst verschenkst du vielleicht Punkte.*

I True or false?

	true	false
1. All the Smugglers were bad, violent men who were very dangerous and had often spent time in prison. Many smugglers were ordinary men who were only trying to earn money or have things such as whiskey or tobacco that they could not buy. Others were well-liked.	☐	☒
2. The first smugglers were called 'owlers'.	☒	☐
3. It was fairly easy for the army to catch smugglers. Smugglers used fast ships and knew the coast well. They were able to hide their goods and after a while they started using weapons to fight the army. It was hard to catch them.	☐	☒
4. Edward I caused the first smuggling to happen when he put tax on wool.	☒	☐

5. Many people hated smugglers and told the army about them. ☐ ☒
   No, ordinary people liked smugglers and saw them as heroes. They didn't tell the army about them very often.
6. Smuggling stopped in the 20th century. ☐ ☒
   Smuggling is still going on today.
7. Smugglers were well able to hide the goods they smuggled. ☒ ☐

II Questions on the text

1. Johnston was a well-liked smuggler like many other smugglers were. He knew the south coast of England very well. Most smugglers knew the coast well. He got a lot of money, spent time in prison and also suffered injuries while smuggling. These things all made him typical of the smugglers who lived back then.
2. The makers of illegal whiskey paid no tax on it and it wasn't as good or as healthy as whiskey produced in factories.

Notenschlüssel:

1	2	3	4	5	6
16–14	13–11	10–9	8–7	6–4	3–0

Test 18
Schwerpunkte: *Relative pronouns, vocabulary*

15 minutes

I Relative pronouns (10 pts.)

Fill in the missing pronoun.

1. I once met a woman __________________ had been to see the Prince of Wales.
2. The film ______________________ we watched last evening was called *Bee Movie*.
3. The shop ______________________ was destroyed by a bomb yesterday was a greengrocer's.
4. I don't like footballers ______________________ try and get other players booked.
5. Do you know J. K. Rowling, the author ______________ wrote the *Harry Potter* novels?

II Opposites (7 pts.)

Give the opposite of these words:

1. safety ________________________________
2. (to) whisper ________________________________
3. familiar ________________________________
4. expensive ________________________________
5. exciting ________________________________
6. (to) agree with ________________________________
7. friend ________________________________

III Word formation (6 pts.)

Find a noun from the same word family. (Example: *to drive* → *driver*)

1. different: ________________
2. (to) smuggle: ________________
3. (to) describe: ________________

IV Give synonyms (2 pts.)

1. Something which is worth a lot of money ________________
2. England, Scotland and Wales ___________________

Solution

I Relative pronouns

1. I once met a woman **who/that** had been to see the Prince of Wales.
2. The film **that/which** we attended last evening was called *Bee Movie*.
3. The shop **which/that** was destroyed by a bomb yesterday was a greengrocer's.
4. I dislike footballers **who** try and get other players booked.
5. Do you know J. K. Rowling, the author **who** wrote the *Harry Potter* novels?

II Opposites

1. danger
2. (to) shout
3. strange, unfamiliar
4. cheap
5. boring
6. (to) disagree with
7. enemy

III Word formation

1. difference
2. smuggler
3. description

IV Give synonyms

1. valuable
2. Great Britain

Notenschlüssel:

1	2	3	4	5	6
25–23	22–20	19–17	16–13	12–10	9–0

Test 19
Schwerpunkt: *Tenses*

20 minutes

I Pictures

(8 pts.)

Look at each of these pictures. Then complete the sentences in line with the example.

Example:

Veronica had been dancing when her telephone suddenly rang.

1. ______________________________

____

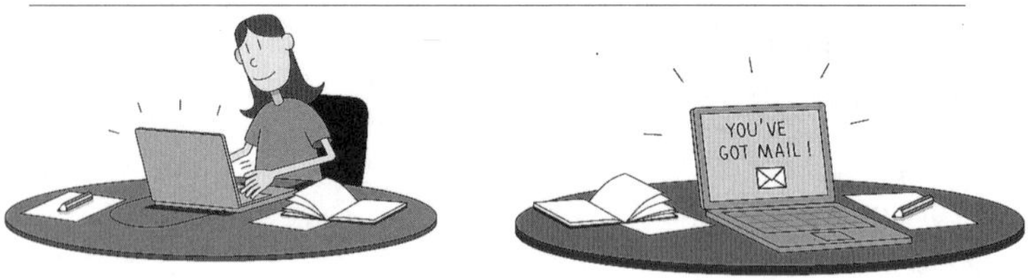

2. ______________________________

____

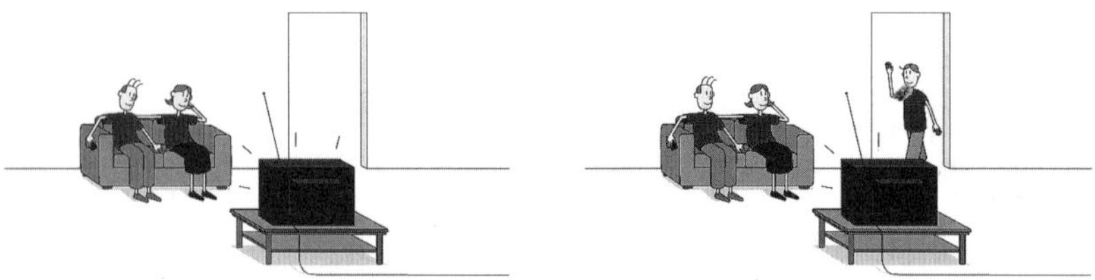

3. ____

____

4. ____

____

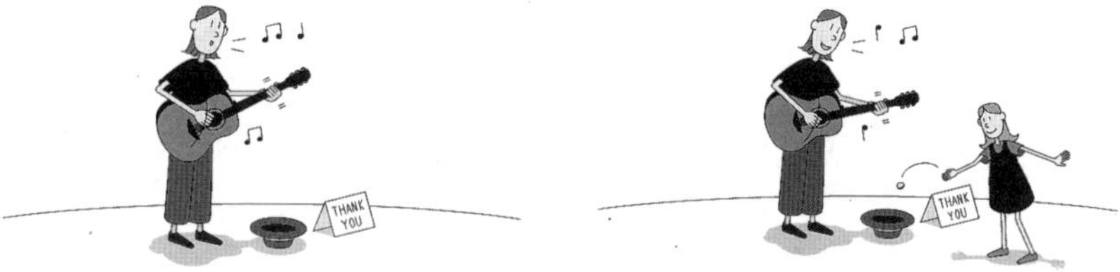

II Tenses (17 pts.)

Fill in the right form of the *simple past* or other tenses in the past. The following text is about William Mulchinock. He wrote *The Rose of Tralee* – one of Ireland's most famous tunes.

1. William Mulchinock ______________ (to write) many songs and ballads before he ______________________ (to decide) to write *The Rose of Tralee*.
2. According to some people, his parents ________________ (not, to like) a girl called Mary O'Connor who he __________ (to fall) in love with some time before so his father and mother ________________ (to sent) him to France.
3. Years later he ____________________ (to return) to Tralee and ___________ (to notice) a funeral coming down the road.
4. After he ____________________ (to stand) there for a while he ____________ (to ask) somebody who the dead person was and the person ___________ (to tell) him it was Mary.

5. William _____________ (to be) so sad he _______________ (to go) home straight away and wrote *The Rose of Tralee* in memory of Mary.
6. After he ____________________ (to live) for a few years in Tralee William _____________ (to leave) for New York.
7. After he _____________________ (to work) in America for six years Mulchinock ________________ (to come back) to Ireland where he _____________ (to die) in 1864.

Solution

__Hinweise:__ Für beide Aufgaben musst die Verwendung und Bildung der Zeiten im Englischen sicher beherrschen. Falls du noch Probleme hast, sieh dir die Regeln in der Kurzgrammatik S. 15–21 noch einmal genau an.

I Pictures

1. Mary had been working at the computer when she received an e-mail.
2. John's parents had been watching TV when he walked in.
3. The boys had been playing football when the dog ran off with the ball.
4. The busker had been singing a song when the young girl threw money into his hat.

II Tenses

1. William Mulchinock **had written** many songs and ballads before he **decided** to write *The Rose of Tralee*.
2. According to some people, his parents **did not like** a girl called Mary O'Connor who he **had fallen** in love with some time before so his father and mother **sent** him to France.
3. Years later he **was returning** to Tralee and **noticed** a funeral coming down the road.
4. After he **had stood/had been standing** there for a while he **asked** somebody who the dead person was and the person **told** him it was Mary.
5. William **was** so sad he **went** home straight away and wrote *The Rose of Tralee* in memory of Mary.
6. After he **had lived/had been living** for a few years in Tralee William **left** for New York.
7. After he **had worked** in America for six years Mulchinock **came back** to Ireland again where he **died** in 1864.

Notenschlüssel:

1	2	3	4	5	6
25–21	20–17	16–14	13–12	11–9	8–0

Test 20
Schwerpunkte: *Reported speech, spelling*

15 minutes

I Reported speech: A letter from Alaska (12 pts.)

Jenny has gone to Alaska and is staying with friends. Yesterday she sent this letter to her best friend Mary. Mary then tells her mother all the news. Use *reported speech* to describe what Mary told her mother. Use as many different verbs as you can.

Dear Mary

I'm having a great time here in Alaska. The weather is cold but dry. We had a little snow last Tuesday but it's lovely weather now. My friends collected me at the airport. They took me to a café for a bite to eat. This week I went into town and bought some presents for my mother and I have already packed them in my suitcase. I'm going to buy some videos later. You may not believe me and I can laugh about it now but I got lost twice when in town. I'll never do that again. My friends gave me a map of the town last night! Later we are going to the movies and afterwards we will have an ice-cream. I will see you soon!

Bye for now

Jenny

II Spelling (8pts.)

Fill in the gaps in the following sentences using a form of one of the following words: *useful, to slip, big, hot, easy, to rub, to taste, to swim.*

1. The ________________ day this summer was the 23rd of July.
2. Kevin is the ________________ boy in his class.
3. The girl ________________ on the ice and broke her foot.
4. Mary made a very ________________ soup for the boy to eat.

5. A good hammer is a very ________________ thing to have if you want to break stones.
6. Question 3 was the ______________ question in the Maths test.
7. Tom started a fire by ________________ two sticks together.
8. John went ________________ in the pool every day last week.

Solution

I Reported speech: A letter from Alaska

Mary told her mother that Jenny was having a great time in Alaska. She said that the weather was cold but dry. She mentioned that they had had a little snow the Tuesday before but that the sun was shining at that moment. She told her mother that Jenny's friends had collected her at the airport and had taken her to a café for a bite to eat. She said she had gone into town that week and had bought some presents for her mother. She mentioned she had already packed them in her suitcase. She said she was going to buy some videos later. She related that she could laugh about it now but she had got lost twice when in town. She said she would never do that again. She told her mother that Jenny's friends had given her a map of the town the night before. She said she would be going to the movies later that day and afterwards she would have an ice-cream. Finally she said that she would see me soon.

II Spelling

1. The **hottest** day this summer was the 23rd of July.
2. Kevin is the **biggest** boy in his class.
3. The girl **slipped** on the ice and broke her foot.
4. Mary made a very **tasty** soup for the boy to eat.
5. A good hammer is a very **useful** thing to have if you want to break stones.
6. Question 3 was the **easiest** question in the Maths test.
7. Tom started a fire by **rubbing** two sticks together.
8. John went **swimming** in the pool every day last week.

Notenschlüssel:

1	2	3	4	5	6
20–18	17–15	14–12	11–10	9–8	7–0

Test 21
Schwerpunkt: *Mediation*

15 minutes

Mediation (30 pts.)

Rita from Scotland and Petra from Germany are on holiday together in England. They meet Stefan, a friend of Petra's. Stefan speaks very little English and Rita doesn't speak German. Therefore Petra has to interpret. Pretend you are Petra.

1. RITA: Can you ask Stefan if he knows his way around London?

   PETRA: ____

2. STEFAN: Ich kenne mich überhaupt nicht aus, aber ich habe einen guten Stadtplan.

   PETRA: ____

3. RITA: Ask him if he has ever been to Kew Gardens.

   PETRA: ____

4. STEFAN: Wo? In Kew Gardens? Kenne ich nicht. Frag Rita was genau Kew Gardens ist.

   PETRA: ____

5. RITA: But he must have heard of them. It's a fantastic place and they even make television programmes about it.

   PETRA: ____

6. STEFAN: Nein, tut mir leid, kenne ich nicht.

   PETRA: ____

7. RITA: Tell him I'll take him there if he buys us dinner.

   PETRA: ____

8. STEFAN: Das würde ich gerne machen. Aber ich habe nur heute Zeit, da ich morgen nach Manchester fahren muss.

   PETRA: ____

9. STEFAN: Gehen wir?

   PETRA: ____

Solution

Hinweise: Bei dieser Übung musst du daran denken, dass es sich hier nicht um eine Übersetzung handelt. Deine Aufgabe ist es, den Sinn des Satzes zu vermitteln. Überlege genau, was gesagt wird und gib diese Informationen weiter. Bei dieser Aufgabe bekommst du 10 Punkte für Inhalt und 20 Punkte für Sprache.

Mediation

1. RITA: Can you ask Stefan if he knows his way around London?
   PETRA: **Stefan, kennst du dich in London aus?**
2. STEFAN: Ich kenne mich überhaupt nicht aus, aber ich habe einen guten Stadtplan.
   PETRA: **He says he doesn't know his way around at all but he has a good map of the city.**
3. RITA: Ask him if he has ever been to Kew Gardens.
   PETRA: **Bist du je in Kew Gardens gewesen?**
4. STEFAN: Wo? In Kew Gardens? Kenne ich nicht. Frag Rita, was genau Kew Gardens ist.
   PETRA: **He doesn't know where it is and I don't think he's ever heard of it. He wants to know what exactly Kew Gardens is.**
5. RITA: But he must have heard of them. It's a fantastic place and they even make television programmes about it.
   PETRA: **Sie sagt du musst davon gehört haben. Es ist ein fantastischer Ort, der sogar oft in Fernsehsendungen vorkommt.**
6. STEFAN: Nein, tut mir leid, kenne ich nicht.
   PETRA: **Sorry, he doesn't know it.**
7. RITA: Tell him I'll take him there if he buys us dinner.
   PETRA: **Rita sagt sie nimmt dich mit dorthin wenn du uns zum Mittagessen einlädst.**
8. STEFAN: Das würde ich gerne machen. Aber ich habe nur heute Zeit, da ich morgen nach Manchester fahren muss.
   PETRA: He would like to do that but he only has time today because he has to go to Manchester tomorrow.
9. STEFAN: Gehen wir?
   PETRA: **Will we go?**

Notenschlüssel:

1	2	3	4	5	6
30–27	26–23	22–19	18–15	14–10	9–0

Test 22
Schwerpunkte: *Possessive pronouns, vocabulary*

10 minutes

I Possessive pronouns (13 pts.)

After a school dance a number of coats get mixed up in the hall of the school. Mr O'Neill is in charge of the coats and he is speaking to John. Fill in the blanks.

1. MR O'NEILL: So tell me John is any of these coats __________?
2. JOHN: That's difficult to say. This brown coat looks a little bit like ______________ coat. Let me look at it a bit closer.
3. JOHN: No, I don't think so. ____________ is much heavier than this one. It actually looks like Barbara's.
4. MR O'NEILL Maybe it is ________________. I'll ask her later.
5. JOHN: You're right. I heard that ________ coat is missing too.
6. MR O'NEILL: Look there she is now. Let's ask ____________.
7. MR O'NEILL: Barbara is this ____________ coat by any chance?
8. BARBARA: No, I think it's Mr Smith's coat. Yes, I'm certain it's ____________.
9. MR O'NEILL: Will you tell ________ he can collect ________ coat here up until ten o'clock this evening?
10. BARBARA: What about __________, John. Have you found it yet?
11. JOHN: I just remembered. I think I left ____________ in our classroom. Let me go and see if it's still there.
12. MR O'NEILL: Oh dear! By the time all the students have __________ coats again I'll be an old man.

II Vocabulary (12 pts.)

Read each definition and then write down the word.

1. A place where pigs are fed: ______________________________
2. You use this on a brush to colour something: ________________
3. North, South, East or West: ______________________
4. It is written on walls and has to be cleaned off: ______________
5. Another word for to swap: ______________________
6. If one country controls many parts of the world we say it rules an ________________.
7. If something is not needed it is ____________________.
8. It keeps our houses warm and uses pipes and radiators to do so: _________________________
9. Another word for dirty clothes: _______________________
10. When the landscape or countryside is beautiful we often use this word: _________________________
11. A habit or a tradition that people have done for many years: ________________________
12. The opposite of narrow: ________________________

Solution

I Possessive pronouns

1. MR O'NEILL: So tell me John is any of these coats **yours**?
2. JOHN: That's difficult to say. This brown coat looks a little bit like **my** coat. Let me look at it a bit closer.
3. JOHN: No, I don't think so. **Mine** is much heavier than this one. It actually looks like Barbara's.
4. MR O'NEILL: Maybe it is **hers**. I'll ask her later.
5. JOHN: You're right. I heard that **her** coat is missing too.
6. MR O'NEILL: Look there she is now. Let's ask **her**.
7. MR O'NEILL: Barbara is this **your** coat by any chance?
8. BARBARA: No, I think it's Mr Smith's coat. Yes, I'm certain it's **his**.
9. MR O NEILL: Will you tell **him** he can collect **his** coat here up until ten o'clock this evening?
10. BARBARA: What about **yours**, John. Have you found it yet?
11. JOHN: I just remembered. I think I left **mine** in our classroom. Let me go and see if it's still there.
12. MR O NEILL: Oh dear! By the time all the students have **their** coats again I'll be an old man.

II Vocabulary

1. pigsty
2. paint
3. direction
4. graffiti
5. exchange
6. empire
7. unnecessary
8. heating
9. washing
10. scenery
11. custom
12. wide

Notenschlüssel:

1	2	3	4	5	6
25–22	21–18	17–14	13–12	11–9	8–0

Test 23
Schwerpunkt: *Listening comprehension*

20 minutes

Listening comprehension

Joan, who lives in Florida, could hardly believe the news when she heard that there had been a tornado in London. Because she has a brother living there she decided to ring him to make sure everything was okay.

I Multiple choice (16 pts.)

Select the correct answer from the following options.

1. Martin lives
   - two streets away from where the tornado struck. ☐
   - quite near where the tornado struck. ☐
   - in a different part of the city. ☐
   - thirty miles from where the tornado struck. ☐
   - in a different town to where the tornado struck. ☐
2. The number of houses hit by the storm was
   - about one hundred and twenty. ☐
   - forty-four. ☐
   - twenty. ☐
   - nobody knows. ☐
   - The BBC says it thinks about eighty houses were hit. ☐
3. Where Joan lives hurricanes usually start
   - off the coast of Ireland. ☐
   - near South Africa. ☐
   - in the Caribbean. ☐
   - at sea. ☐
   - along the Florida coast. ☐

4. Hurricane Andrew destroyed
   - Joan's house and garden. ☐
   - Joan's neighbour's house. ☐
   - Joan's garage. ☐
   - Joan's holiday home. ☐
5. Britain experiences about
   - five tornadoes a year. ☐
   - no tornadoes. ☐
   - over sixty tornadoes. ☐
   - thirty-five tornadoes a year. ☐
   - a huge number of tornadoes. ☐
6. Tornadoes in Britain usually happen in
   - towns like Halifax or Bradford. ☐
   - London and the south of England. ☐
   - in areas where there are many towns. ☐
   - in areas where there are only small villages. ☐
   - Scotland. ☐
7. Martin, Joan's brother, is
   - married with no children. ☐
   - an unmarried man. ☐
   - married with children. ☐
   - a man whose wife died two years ago. ☐
   - divorced. ☐

II Question on the text (6 pts.)

Summarise in your own words the kind of damage the London tornado caused.

____

____

____

____

____

Solution

Hinweise: *Einige Wörter hier sind vielleicht neu für dich: „measured", „damage" und „rural". Du kannst dir den Text auch ruhig mehrmals anhören. Es ist hilfreich, wenn du dir beim Hören Notizen machst.*

Listening comprehension

Joan, who lives in Florida, could hardly believe the news when she heard that there had been a tornado in London. Because she has a brother living there she decided to ring him to make sure everything was okay.

MARTIN: Hello?

JOAN: Hi Martin. This is Joan speaking. How are you all?

MARTIN: Fine thanks.

JOAN: I saw on the television there's been a tornado in your part of the world. Are you all okay?

MARTIN: Yes Joan we're fine. That happened yesterday in North London. In a place called Kensel Rise. That's more than thirty miles away from where we are.

JOAN: Oh thanks be to God. I was so worried I couldn't sleep when I went to bed so I decided to phone.

MARTIN: That's nice of you, but we're all fine. Don't worry. Mind you, the pictures on the telly were horrific. People had to leave their homes, roofs were blown off, windows shattered and record wind speeds were measured. They've closed off the streets where it happened and have provided emergency shelter for many families. I heard one man on the BBC say he thought the world was coming to an end. He was very frustrated because he lost his whole sitting-room.

JOAN: Dreadful isn't it? How many homes were hit by the storm?

MARTIN: About one hundred as far as I know and they think about twenty of these houses can no longer be lived in. They'll have to be knocked down.

JOAN: Oh dear! We have hurricanes all the time here. They usually start somewhere in the Caribbean and they get stronger as they move across the sea. I remember when Hurricane Andrew struck I thought we'd lose the whole house but in the end only our garage was damaged.

MARTIN: Well as far as I know there are about thirty-five tornadoes a year in Britain but most of them happen in rural areas so they don't do much damage. This one happened in London which is why everybody is talking about it.

JOAN: Well it's nice to hear you're all safe and well. Give my regards to Helen and the children.

MARTIN: Yes I will and thanks again for calling.

I Multiple choice

1. Martin lives

   - two streets away from where the tornado struck. ☐
   - quite near where the tornado struck. ☐
   - in a different part of the city. ☐
   - thirty miles from where the tornado struck. ☒
   - in a different town to where the tornado struck. ☐

2. The number of houses hit by the storm was

   - about one hundred twenty. ☒
   - forty-four. ☐
   - twenty. ☐
   - nobody knows. ☐
   - The BBC says it thinks about eighty houses were hit. ☐

3. Where Joan lives hurricanes usually start

   - off the coast of Ireland. ☐
   - near South Africa. ☐
   - in the Caribbean. ☒
   - at sea. ☐
   - along the Florida coast. ☐

4. Hurricane Andrew destroyed

   - Joan's house and garden. ☐
   - Joan's neighbour's house. ☐
   - Joan's garage. ☒
   - Joan's holiday home. ☐

5. Britain experiences about

   - five tornadoes a year. ☐
   - no tornadoes. ☐
   - over sixty tornadoes. ☐
   - thirty-five tornadoes a year. ☒
   - a huge number of tornadoes. ☐

6. Tornadoes in Britain usually happen in
   - towns like Halifax or Bradford. ☐
   - London and the south of England. ☐
   - in areas where there are many towns. ☐
   - in areas where there are only small villages. ☒
   - Scotland. ☐
7. Martin, Joan's brother, is
   - married with no children. ☐
   - an unmarried man. ☐
   - married with children. ☒
   - a man whose wife died two years ago. ☐
   - divorced. ☐

II Question on the text

There was a lot of damage done by the storm. Houses lost their roofs, glass was broken and one man lost his sitting room. Over one hundred houses were hit by the storm and many people had to leave their homes.

Notenschlüssel:

1	2	3	4	5	6
22–20	19–17	16–14	13–11	10–8	7–0

Test 24
Schwerpunkte: *Countries, reported speech, synonyms*

15 minutes

I Countries: Fill in the missing adjectives (9 pts.)

1. The adjective that we get from the country known as Hungary. Budapest is the ________________ capital city.

2. Thailand, Korea and Vietnam are all ________________ countries.
3. Amsterdam is a ________________ city.
4. What kind of cross can you see in this picture? A ________________ cross.
5. 'Ciao' is an ________________ word.
6. Arnold Schwarzenegger is __________ by birth but he is an ________________ politician.
7. Cardiff is the ________________ capital.
8. People in Finland speak ____________.
9. Geneva is a ________________ city.

II Reported speech (14 pts.)

Your task is to put these sentences into *reported speech.*

1. "I am working in San Francisco," Susan said.

____

____

2. "I took a little money with me," Mary replied.

____

____

3. "Pat and Geraldine liked the party," Jimmy mentioned.

____

____

4. "I was washing myself when you called," Helen said.

____

____

5. "We can't go with you to the game," Barry said.

____

____

6. Sara shouted, "I'll see you on Saturday."

____

____

7. Mike told Peter, "I must save my money for my journey to Alaska."

____

____

III Synonyms (3 pts.)

Give a different word with the same meaning for the underlined words:

1. He <u>said no</u> when I said England is a lovely country:

   He ________________.

2. <u>The number of people</u> in a country: ______________________

3. <u>To say "damn"</u> or something worse when you are angry:

   ____

Solution

I Countries: Fill in the missing adjectives

1. The adjective that we get from the country known as Hungary. Budapest is the **Hungarian** capital city.
2. Thailand, Korea and Vietnam are all **Asian** countries.
3. Amsterdam is a **Dutch** city.
4. What kind of cross can you see in this picture? A **Celtic** cross.
5. Ciao is an **Italian** word.
6. Arnold Schwarzenegger is **Austrian** by birth but he is an **American** politician.
7. Cardiff is the **Welsh** capital.
8. People in Finland speak **Finnish**.
9. Geneva is a **Swiss** city.

II Reported speech

1. Susan told me that she was working in San Francisco.
2. Mary replied that she had taken a little money with her.
3. Jimmy mentioned that Pat and Geraldine had liked the party.
4. Helen said that she had been washing herself when I called.
5. Barry said they couldn't go with me to the game.
6. Sara shouted that she would see me on Saturday.
7. Mike told Peter that he had to save his money for his journey to Alaska.

III Synonyms

1. disagreed
2. population
3. (to) curse

Notenschlüssel:

1	2	3	4	5	6
26–24	23–20	19–17	16–14	13–11	10–0

Test 25
Schwerpunkt: *Reading comprehension*

20 minutes

Reading comprehension

The Californian Gold Rush

As a carpenter the last thing James Marshall expected to find while working at a saw mill[1] near the American River in California was gold. The year was 1848, the same year America took California from Mexico. Marshall later said that he made the gold discovery while checking a millwheel. He saw something shiny, caught behind a stone beneath the water. When he showed his boss John Sutter, the owner of the mill, what he had found, Sutter exclaimed "It's gold – at least twenty-three-carat gold." Today we have very little exact information about Marshall's discovery. He himself was never very sure of the date. He later felt that he had made the discovery "on or about the 19th of January" but both San Francisco's weekly newspapers mentioned it in March 1848. Nothing more happened until a young shopkeeper called Sam Brannan understood that there was money to be made from a gold rush. He bought products for his shop that he knew would be needed by men searching for gold. Then he travelled to San Francisco with a bottle of gold dust[2] in one hand and shouted "Gold! I have gold from the American River!" Soon people were rushing to the American River. The local newspapers said this was not a good thing because the whole country, from San Francisco to Los Angeles and from the sea shore to Sierra Nevada, was sick with gold fever and people were leaving their work in the field or the houses they were building to go look for gold. During the summer of 1848, about 6,000 "forty-eighters" arrived at the gold fields. The rush to California's goldfields got worse during the winter and early spring of 1849. Hundreds of towns sprang to life in California during the gold rush. Wherever gold was discovered, mining camps appeared almost overnight. Some disappeared just as quickly, once the easy gold was gone. The greatest boom town of all was San Francisco. Its population grew from just 600 in 1848 to 25,000 in 1849. A man from New York called Matthew Taylor arrived in San Francisco in September 1849. Later he remembered "hundreds of tents and houses along the shore for over a mile. A strong wind was blowing through a gap in the hills, filling the streets with clouds of dust. On every side stood buildings of all kinds, begun or half-finished, open in front and covered with all kinds of signs in all languages. The streets were full of people, hurrying here and there. I didn't know if I was awake or in some wonderful dream."

Annotations
1 *saw mill*: Sägewerk; 2 *dust*: Staub

I True or false?

(8 pts)

	true	false
The gold Marshall found was high quality gold.	☐	☐
Marshall knew exactly when he found the gold.	☐	☐
Sam Brannan was a good businessman.	☐	☐
The towns that sprang up during the gold rush became very big and are still alive today.	☐	☐

II Questions on the text

(16 pts.)

1. Is it true to say that James Marshall was looking for the gold he found? Why (not)?

____

____

____

2. Explain how Marshall's discovery turned into a Gold Rush.

____

____

____

3. What strange things were men doing because of the gold?

____

____

____

____

4. What kind of town was San Francisco at this time.
   Describe it in your own words.

____

____

____

Solution

I True or false?

	true	false
The gold Marshall found was high quality gold.	✗	
Marshall knew exactly when he found the gold.		✗
Sam Brannan was a good businessman.	✗	
The towns that sprang up during the gold rush became very big and are still alive today.		✗

II Questions on the text

1. This is not true. He was working on a millwheel when he found the gold by accident. He was not looking for gold.
2. Nothing happened for a while but when the newspapers reported it and a man called Brannan saw there was money to be made he travelled to San Francisco and told the news everywhere. Soon people started to come in search of more gold.
3. They were leaving their work unfinished in fields or just going away from the houses they lived in. They travelled in search of something even though they had no idea if they would find it. Many of them were doing this in the hope of a better life but in truth they were ill with gold fever. They lived in tents for a long time and put up with a hard life that they would normally not have put up with.
4. It was a windswept place full of tents everywhere and many people coming and going in search of their dream – gold.

Notenschlüssel:

1	2	3	4	5	6
24–22	21–19	18–16	15–12	11–10	9–0

Test 26
Schwerpunkt: *Listening comprehension*

15 minutes

Listening comprehension

Michael James and Helen Cross are having a discussion about hobbies.

I Multiple choice (20 pts.)

1. Michael and Helen are talking about
   - their plans for the summer holidays. ☐
   - living in the city of Quebec. ☐
   - the kind of things they like doing in their free time. ☐
   - their favourite subjects at school. ☐

2. Helen
   - is a very good chess *(= Schach)* player who has won many competitions. ☐
   - plays chess but only for fun. ☐
   - got a present of a chessboard from her mother. ☐
   - plays chess in a club. ☐

3. Helen was taught how to knit *(= stricken)*
   - by her mother at home. ☐
   - by her sister at home. ☐
   - by her grandmother. ☐
   - by a teacher at school. ☐

4. Helen's mother and father think that horse-riding
   - is very dangerous. ☐
   - is very expensive. ☐
   - should only be for girls. ☐
   - is an interesting hobby. ☐

5. When Helen goes travelling she finds out as much as she can about
   - the cost of the trip. ☐
   - the weather there. ☐
   - the local language. ☐
   - historic sites to go to. ☐
6. Michael would go
   - snowboarding with Helen. ☐
   - playing chess with Helen. ☐
   - on holiday with Helen. ☐
   - horse-riding with Helen. ☐

II True or false? (8 pts.)

Say whether these are true or false.
If they are false give the reason why.

		true	false
1.	Helen wants a horse of her own.	☐	☐
	______________________________		
2.	Helen has very few hobbies.	☐	☐
	______________________________		
3.	Helen can do all her hobbies the whole year round.	☐	☐
	______________________________		
4.	Helen has only got pen-pals in Manchester.	☐	☐
	______________________________		

Solution

Listening comprehension

Hinweis: *Kennst du schon Wörter wie „trophies", „show-off" und „knitting"? Wenn nicht, schaue nach ob du im Wörterbuch eine Erklärung finden kannst.*

Hobbies

Michael James and Helen Cross are having a discussion about hobbies.

MICHAEL: What are your favourite hobbies Helen? What do you like doing in your spare time?

HELEN: That's not as easy a question as it sounds, Michael. There are many, many things I like doing. I have outdoor and indoor hobbies and then there are some things I do at certain times of the year that I would also call hobbies. Which shall I talk about?

MICHAEL: Oh you are a bit of a show-off. Go on then tell me about your indoor hobbies first.

HELEN: Well, I love playing chess. My mother taught me how to play when I was young and she is in the same chess club as I am. I've won many competitions and trophies so it is one of the main things that I like doing. Apart from that I love knitting even if it is a bit old-fashioned and not very cool.

MICHAEL: Knitting! Are you serious?

HELEN: Of course I am.

MICHAEL: Who taught you knitting? Your mother I suppose?

HELEN: No actually. I learned to knit at school.

MICHAEL: That's only a girl's hobby. That wouldn't be anything for me.

HELEN: I do like doing other things such as watching TV, reading and writing to my pen-pals.

MICHAEL: How many pen-pals have you got?

HELEN: Two. One in Manchester and the other in Quebec. We write to each other every week and telephone once a month. For my outdoor hobbies I like swimming, diving and hiking. I go for a ride on a horse twice a month which is great fun. My mother and father don't think so however because it is a bit expensive. One day I'd like to have my very own horse. That's a dream of mine.

MICHAEL: So what kind of hobbies do you have that you only do now and again?

HELEN: Well, I love travelling. We go on holidays as often as we can and I always read up about the historic places to visit beforehand. Last year we went to Canada and had a great time. I visited my friend in Quebec first of all and then went on to Vancouver. It was really interesting to see the school my friend goes to and to go walking in the mountains. The other hobby I only do from time to time is snowboarding. I don't have to explain why I'm sure.

MICHAEL: No you don't! I'm sure you prefer cold winters with lots of snow. That's the only hobby we share. I love snowboarding. You don't play football or Play Station and I hate knitting, swimming and horse-riding. I suppose I would go on holiday with you though. What's the nicest place you've been to for snowboarding?

HELEN: Two years ago my father took me to the Alps. We stayed in a lovely village in Austria and had a super time. The snow was great!

MICHAEL: Well, thank you for telling me about your hobbies. It was very interesting.

HELEN: You're welcome!

I Multiple choice

1. Michael and Helen are talking about
   - their plans for the summer holidays. [ ]
   - living in the city of Quebec. [ ]
   - the kind of things they like doing in their free time. [x]
   - their favourite subjects at school. [ ]
2. Helen
   - is a very good chess player who has won many competitions. [x]
   - plays chess but only for fun. [ ]
   - got a present of a chessboard from her mother. [ ]
   - plays chess in a club. [ ]
3. Helen was taught how to knit
   - by her mother at home. [ ]
   - by her sister at home. [ ]
   - by her grandmother. [ ]
   - by a teacher at school. [x]

4. Helen's mother and father think that horse-riding
   - is very dangerous. ☐
   - is very expensive. ☒
   - should only be for girls. ☐
   - is an interesting hobby. ☐
5. When Helen goes travelling she finds out as much as she can about
   - the cost of the trip. ☐
   - the weather there. ☐
   - the local language. ☐
   - historic sites to go to. ☒
6. Michael would go
   - snowboarding with Helen. ☒
   - playing chess with Helen. ☐
   - on holiday with Helen. ☒
   - horse-riding with Helen. ☐

II True or false?

		true	false
1.	Helen wants a horse of her own.	☒	☐
2.	Helen has very few hobbies. This is false. She has a lot of hobbies.	☐	☒
3.	Helen can do all her hobbies the whole year round. This is false because she can only go snowboarding in the winter.	☐	☒
4.	Helen has only got pen-pals in Manchester. No she doesn't. She also writes to a friend in Quebec.	☐	☒

Notenschlüssel:

1	2	3	4	5	6
28–25	24–21	20–18	17–14	13–12	11–0

Klassenarbeit 1

Schwerpunkte: ***Listening comprehension, vocabulary, composition***

45 minutes

I Listening comprehension

Listen to the text about the two friends, Conchita and Stephanie.

A Multiple choice (10 pts.)

Mark the correct answer(s).

1. How do we know that the two girls were friends?
   - They lived in the same town. ☐
   - They played together and went walking together. ☐
   - Their fathers were friends. ☐
   - They sat beside each other at school. ☐
2. Conchita was different to Stephanie because
   - she was a better-looking girl. ☐
   - her father was not as rich as Stephanie's. ☐
   - their fathers were from different places in America. ☐
   - Conchita's mother spoke no English. ☐
3. Stephanie's mother had worked as a
   - dentist. ☐
   - nurse. ☐
   - vet (a doctor for animals). ☐
   - model. ☐
4. In order to get help Conchita
   - told her mother to ring the vet. ☐
   - used her mobile phone to ring for help. ☐
   - used a telephone box to call the vet. ☐
   - sent a smoke signal. ☐

5. Stephanie's father was

   a banker. ☐

   a tour guide. ☐

   a vet. ☐

   a camera man. ☐

B Questions on the text (10 pts.)

Answer in full English sentences.

1. Give two reasons why Conchita thought the bird was drunk.

   ____

   ____

   ____

2. How did the vet say the birds were getting drunk?

   ____

   ____

3. Do you think it was right that Stephanie was not interviewed for the news? Explain why.

   ____

   ____

   ____

C Summary (4 pts.)

Explain in English why saving the bird's life was to be important for Conchita and what she later became.

____

____

____

II Vocabulary

A Word formation (3 pts.)

Find a word from the same word family.

regular *(adjective)*: ______________ *(adverb)*

sun *(noun)*: ______________ *(adjective)*

(to) use *(verb)*: ______________ *(adjective)*

B Synonyms (3 pts.)

Give a different word with the same meaning for the underlined words.

1. He said yes. He ___________________.
2. We went away from the house. We _____________________ the house.
3. I can't help you now. I can't help you ___________________.

C Verbs (20 pts.)

Put in the correct forms of the verbs and some prepositions and pronouns.

Terry and Joan _______________ (to go) shopping in Bristol last week. First Terry _______________ (to buy) a green blouse, then she ____________ (to see) trousers, but Joan _______________ (not, to think) much __________. Then Joan _____________ (to find) a present for her mum: she _________________ (to hear) a nice song in a CD shop. She _______________ (to call) out: "Hey, that's super! Mum likes that song. This band _______________ (to play) in London last month!" So Joan _________________ (to take) the CD and ______________ (to pay) ___________ it.

But __________________________________ (two girls, to meet) Eric and Nick in the city? – No, they ______________________, they ______________ (to know) that the boys _____________ (to be) in the city, but they _______________________ (not, to sit) in the same café, so they ________________________ (not, to see) them. Later they _______________ (to meet) Joan's father and he _______________ (to drive) them home.

III Composition (24 pts.)

Imagine you are Conchita. Write a dialogue of 150–200 words that takes place during your TV interview. Think of the kind of questions a person might ask a girl in this situation and then begin.

Solution

I Listening comprehension

Hinweis: *Schwierige Vokabeln in diesem Text sind: „crew“, „appearance“, „cage“. Es ist hilfreich, wenn du dir beim zweiten Hören Notizen machst.*

The Story of Conchita, Stephanie and the drunken bird

Conchita and Stephanie were very good friends. They sat beside each other at school, played in the afternoon, and often went out together at the weekend. Conchita was a quiet, very beautiful-looking girl with long black hair and brown eyes. She loved animals and listening to pop music. Stephanie had blonde hair and was very clever in school but she wasn't very pretty. Yet Stephanie, whose father was a banker, often told Conchita that one day she would be a model or a film star. "My mother has worked as a model and I will too. You wait and see!" Stephanie never seemed to realize that Conchita, who was a little shy and whose father was a caretaker in a school, was actually far more beautiful and much more likely to become a model or a star than she was. One evening the two girls were walking down by the beach. Above them the cars passed by on the highway. Suddenly the two girls saw a white seabird on the beach and both girls knew there was something wrong. The bird was not able to walk properly and it seemed as if it was going to fall down at any moment. "The poor bird," Conchita said. "Wow!" Stephanie exclaimed "That sure is one sick bird!" "I think that bird is drunk," Conchita replied. "Drunk! Don't be silly Conchita! Have you ever heard of a drunken bird?" "Well, there have been stories in the paper." It was at that moment that Conchita decided she would have to get help for the bird because it was clearly in trouble. "Come on, let's finish our walk," Stephanie said angrily. "The bird will be okay!" But Conchita was already running up the hill to the telephone box. "Stay there! I'll be back in a while," she shouted to her friend. Twenty minutes later Stephanie was getting very tired of looking at the bird when Conchita came down the sandy hill with a woman by her side. An hour later the bird had just been put in a cage when a television crew came rushing down the hill. One of the TV people asked the vet, "Is it really another of the drunken seabirds?" "Yes," said the vet, "the third this week. The birds are eating fish that have been feeding on a food that causes the birds to become drunk when they eat the fish. Seabirds can die from it and this bird would have died if it hadn't been for this girl," she said turning to Conchita. "Well, it makes a great news story. And what a pretty girl we have here," the lady said. "Can I ask you a few questions?" "I was there too," Stephanie interrupted, smiling at the lady. "We only need one person, I think. Can you step back a little?" And that is how Conchita came to make the first of her appearances on television telling the whole of America what she had done for the bird.

And years later, long after she had become a famous model, a film star and one of America's most famous faces on TV, she often told people that her career all started when she saved a drunken bird.

A Multiple choice

1. How do we know that the two girls were friends?
   - [ ] They lived in the same town.
   - [x] They played together and went walking together.
   - [ ] Their fathers were friends.
   - [x] They sat beside eacht other at school.
2. Conchita was different to Stephanie because
   - [x] she was a better-looking girl.
   - [x] her father was not as rich as Stephanie's.
   - [ ] their fathers were from different places in America.
   - [ ] Conchita's mother spoke no English.
3. Stephanie's mother had worked as a
   - [ ] dentist.
   - [ ] nurse.
   - [ ] vet (a doctor for animals).
   - [x] model.
4. In order to get help Conchita
   - [ ] told her mother to ring the vet.
   - [ ] used her mobile phone to ring for help.
   - [x] used a telephone box to call the vet.
   - [ ] sent a smoke signal.
5. Stephanie's father was
   - [x] a banker.
   - [ ] a tour guide.
   - [ ] a vet.
   - [ ] a camera man.

B Questions on the text

1. The bird was hardly able to walk and looked as if it would fall down at any moment. She had, however, also heard stories about birds who were drunk.
2. The vet said that the birds had been eating fish that had eaten food that made the birds drunk.
3. Yes I do. Stephanie thought the bird was ill and didn't believe Conchita. Stephanie wanted to keep going and leave the bird where they had found it. She was not interested in saving the animal so it was only right that she should not be interviewed.

C Summary

Conchita later became a TV star and model. She was one of America's best-known faces. She often said that she got her start in television the day she rescued a bird on the beach that appeared to be drunk. Afterwards she was interviewed by a reporter and that gave her the first taste of being a star and being on television. She liked it so much she made a career out of it.

II Vocabulary

A Word formation

1. regularly
2. sunny
3. useful

B Synonyms

1. He **agreed**.
2. We **left** the house.
3. I can't help you **at the moment**.

C Verbs

Terry and Joan **went** shopping in Bristol last week. First Terry **bought** a green blouse, then she **saw** trousers, but Joan **didn't think** much **of them**. Then Joan **found** a present for her mum: she **heard** a nice song in a CD shop. She **called** out: "Hey, that's super! Mum likes that song. This band **played** in London last month!" So Joan **took** the CD and **paid for** it. But **did the two girls meet** Eric and Nick in the city? – No, they **didn't**, they **knew** that the boys **were** in the city, but they **didn't sit** in the same café, so they **didn't see** them. Later they **met** Joan's father and he **drove** them home.

III Composition

Hinweise: *Bei dieser Aufgabe ist es wichtig, dass du dich in die Rolle des Mädchens hineinversetzt. Was hat Conchita gesehen? Was hat sie getan, um den Vogel zu retten? Wie lange hat es gedauert bis Hilfe kam? Wie hat sie sich gefühlt? Beschreibe ihre Gefühle so genau wie möglich. Überlege, was ein Reporter fragen würde. Wenn du all dies in deinen Dialog integriert hast und außerdem darauf geachtet hast, gesprochenes Englisch zu verwenden, darfst du dir 8 Punkte für den Inhalt geben.*

INTERVIEWER: Well we are here at the beach where another drunken bird has been found and rescued. The girl who helped save the bird is right beside me. Will you tell us something about yourself?

CONCHITA: Hello. My name is Conchita and I live here in the area.

INTERVIEWER: So how did you come to find the bird?

CONCHITA: My friend Stephanie and I often go for a walk here along the beach after school. Today as we were walking along I saw a bird who was behaving in a very strange way, it wasn't even able to walk properly. At first I couldn't believe my eyes but then I remembered hearing something on the news about drunken birds. I felt so sorry for the bird I just had to do something.

INTERVIEWER: So what did you do then?

CONCHITA: I ran up to the highway to a place where I knew there's a phone and I called for help.

INTERVIEWER: How long did that take?

CONCHITA: I guess the vet got here fifteen minutes afterwards.

INTERVIEWER: So what did he say then?

CONCHITA: He said I saved the bird's life which really made my day. I'd hate to think the bird would have died if we had done nothing. It was a great feeling knowing we'd saved the bird.

INTERVIEWER: What will all your friends at school say when they hear the news?

CONCHITA: I think they'll be quite surprised to see me. They'll all want to hear the full story I guess.

INTERVIEWER: Well thanks very much for talking to us Conchita and there you have it folks, the girl who saved a drunken bird. Back to you Bill in the studio.

Notenschlüssel:

1	2	3	4	5	6
74–66	65–57	56–48	47–39	38–30	29–0

Klassenarbeit 2

Schwerpunkte: ***Listening comprehension, grammar, vocabulary, composition***

45 minutes

I Listening comprehension

Gordon Blair is 34 years old and he works as a teacher. His good friend Kelly Owen is working near Hadrian's Wall. Kelly has invited Gordon to bring his class for a tour of the site and they are now discussing what they have seen.

A Multiple choice (18 pts.)

Listen to the text and mark the correct answer.
More than one answer may be correct.

1. Gordon Blair works as
   - a language teacher in Northumberland. ☐
   - a history teacher in Northumberland. ☐
   - an archaeologist at Hadrian's Wall. ☐
   - a history teacher in Durham. ☐
2. Hadrian came to Britain
   - to find out why the Scots had not been beaten. ☐
   - to meet the Scots. ☐
   - to bring new soldiers for the battle against the Scots. ☐
   - to congratulate his soldiers. ☐
3. According to the text the Romans built 1,000 miles of road
   - soon after invading Britain. ☐
   - in twenty-five years. ☐
   - over a long period of time. ☐
   - as fast as they possibly could. ☐
4. The main job Roman soldiers had to do was
   - help build roads. ☐
   - cook meals. ☐
   - defend the Roman Empire. ☐
   - carry weapons *(= Waffen)* from one town to another. ☐

5. At the moment Kelly Owen
   is working as a guide at Hadrian's Wall. ☐
   is working as a history teacher in a local school. ☐
   is working as an archaeologist. ☐
   is working on a Roman road. ☐

6. The Romans ate big meals and often started with
   fish. ☐
   duck. ☐
   African sweet wine cakes. ☐
   leaves and honey. ☐

7. In Roman Britain slaves had
   to cook meals. ☐
   to do the heavy work. ☐
   to work every day of the week. ☐
   to ask permission to speak to a general. ☐

B Question on the text (4 pts.)

Why did the Romans need roads and what did they use them for?

____

____

II Grammar (7 pts.)

Study the following timeline which is written in the *active voice*. Change this timeline to the *passive voice*.

43 AD

1. The Romans invade and take over Britain.

____

43–47 AD

2. They quickly build many new roads.

____

43–410 AD

3. The Romans introduce fish sauce and olive oil to Britain.

____

70 ~ 84 AD

4. The Romans conquer Wales and Scotland.

____

122–133 AD

5. Hadrian orders Roman solidiers to build a wall.

____

155 AD

6. 155 tribes *(= Stämme)* from Scotland attack the Romans.

____

211 AD

7. The Romans control Caledonia (Scotland).

____

III Vocabulary (3 pts.)

In the above timeline which word means

1. (to) bring something new in?

____

2. (to) beat and take over somewhere?

____

3. a group of people with common characteristics (and related to one another)?

____

IV Composition: Writing a telephone conversation (20 pts.)

Imagine you are visiting Britain on a school exchange. You and your classmates are visiting Hadrian's Wall. You are now standing on the wall as shown in this photograph.

Ring a pen pal of yours from London.

Tell him

- where you are,
- when and how you got there,
- who is with you,
- why the wall was built,
- whether you are enjoying the trip and what else you have liked so far in England.

Write a dialogue of about 200 words.

Solution

I Listening comprehension

Hinweis: *Die Vokabeln „trade", „sweet-wine", „invade" und „weapon" sind vielleicht neu für dich.*

At Hadrian's Wall

Gordon Blair is 34 years old and he works as a history teacher at a school in Northumberland. His good friend Kelly Owen is an archaeologist and this summer she is working near Hadrian's Wall. Kelly has invited Gordon to bring his history class for a tour of the site and they are now discussing what they have seen.

KELLY: Well, children, the Romans were in Britain until 410 AD. After the Romans had beaten the English, a Roman army was sent to Scotland. It won a lot of battles but could not beat all of the Scots. The Roman Emperor at the time was called Hadrian. Hadrian came to England to see why his army was not winning the war with the Scots. He then told his men to build a long wall from one side of England to the other to keep out the Scots. This wall became known as Hadrian's Wall.

GORDON: So how long was the wall?

KELLY: We think the wall was 129 kilometres long and was about 3 metres high. Hadrian's Wall was built by soldiers of the Roman army. They lived in forts near the wall. Their job was then to stop any Scottish attacks and help with the building of forts and roads.

GORDON: What exactly are you working on at the moment Kelly?

KELLY: At the moment we are carrying out work on part of a Roman road. Soon after invading Britain the Romans had built over 1,000 miles of roads! They were great road builders.

GORDON: What exactly did they need the roads for? Were the English roads not good enough for them?

KELLY *(laughing)*: No they weren't! English roads were grassy and dirty and you couldn't use them in bad weather. The Romans needed better, straight roads. Straight roads meant they could move quickly to areas of trouble. Roman generals needed good roads so that they could send orders to their soldiers in forts as far away as Hadrian's Wall. Roads were also important for getting food and weapons to the soldiers. In times of peace, good safe roads meant more trade and more trade meant more money for the Emperor.

GORDON: So what did the Roman soldiers who built the roads eat?

KELLY: A Roman meal was very big. They ate food like fish to begin the meal and then they had wild pig or duck for the main meal and hot African sweet-wine cakes to finish. The meal was cooked by the slaves and they did all the heavy work.

GORDON: All this talk of food makes me feel hungry! Let's have lunch!

KELLY: Good idea! Follow me!

A Multiple choice

1. Gordon Blair works as
   - a language teacher in Northumberland. ☐
   - a history teacher in Northumberland. ☒
   - an archaeologist at Hadrian's Wall. ☐
   - a history teacher in Durham. ☐
2. Hadrian came to Britain
   - to find out why the Scots had not been beaten. ☒
   - to meet the Scots. ☐
   - to bring new soldiers for the battle against the Scots. ☐
   - to congratulate his soldiers. ☐
3. According to the text the Romans built 1,000 miles of road
   - soon after invading Britain. ☒
   - in twenty-five years. ☐
   - over a long period of time. ☐
   - as fast as they possibly could. ☐
4. The main job Roman soldiers had to do was
   - help build roads. ☒
   - cook meals. ☐
   - defend the Roman Empire. ☒
   - carry weapons from one town to another. ☐
5. At the moment Kelly Owen
   - is working as a guide at Hadrian's Wall. ☐
   - is working as a history teacher in a local school. ☐
   - is working as an archaeologist. ☒
   - is working on a Roman road. ☒

6. The Romans ate big meals and often started with

   fish. ☒

   duck. ☐

   African sweet wine cakes. ☐

   leaves and honey. ☐

7. In Roman Britain slaves had

   to cook meals. ☒

   to do the heavy work. ☒

   to work every day of the week. ☐

   to ask permission to speak to a general. ☐

B Question on the text

The Romans needed roads in order to get instructions from one place to another and also to move weapons and food from fort to fort.

II Grammar

1. Britain is invaded and taken over by the Romans.
2. Many new roads are quickly built (by them).
3. Fish sauce and olive oil are introduced to Britain by the Romans.
4. Wales and Scotland are conquered by the Romans.
5. Roman solidiers are ordered to build a wall by Hadrian.
6. The Romans are attacked by 155 tribes from Scotland.
7. Caledonia (Scotland) is controlled by the Romans.

III Vocabulary

1. (to) introduce
2. (to) conquer
3. a tribe

IV Composition: Writing a telephone conversation

Hinweis: *Lies die Aufgabenstellung genau durch. Sie gibt an, welche Punkte in deinem Dialog enthalten sein sollen. Nur wenn du alle Informationen eingearbeitet hast, darfst du dir die volle Punktzahl von 8 Punkten für den Inhalt geben. Für jede Information, die du vergessen hast, musst du dir einen Punkt abziehen.*

STEVE: Hello?

YOU: Hi, Steve, this is Tim speaking. How are you?

STEVE: Tim! Great to hear you! I'm fine thanks. How are you?

YOU: Not bad at all. Guess where I am?

STEVE: I've no idea. Tell me.

YOU: I'm standing near Hadrian's Wall. I arrived here yesterday by bus with my class and two of our teachers and it's fantastic. It's just like in our schoolbook.

STEVE: Sounds great.

YOU: The wall is really big and wide. I feel like a Roman soldier when I'm standing on top of it! It was built to keep the Scots out of England and I bet they weren't able to cross it.

STEVE: So what are your plans for the rest of the trip?

YOU: We go on to Newcastle today and spend the night there. It's been super so far and I really loved Liverpool. We went to loads of places where the Beatles played and we were taken into Goodison Park!

STEVE: So will I see you down here in London? I'd take you to see the new Arsenal football stadium. We might even go to a game.

YOU: No, I'm afraid not. But I could come over in the summer if you like.

STEVE: That would be great. See you then! Be sure and e-mail me once you get home.

YOU: Bye for now.

STEVE: Bye.

Notenschlüssel:

1	2	3	4	5	6
52–45	44–37	36–31	30–26	25–20	19–0

Klassenarbeit 3
Schwerpunkte: ***Reading comprehension, vocabulary, grammar, composition***

45 minutes

I Reading comprehension

Learning about sharks[1]

Sharks, who spend their whole lives in water, have been around for over 400 million years and have the most powerful jaws[2] on the planet. Unlike most animals' jaws, both the sharks' upper and lower jaws move. A shark bites with its lower jaw first and then with its upper jaw. A shark may grow and use over 20,000 teeth in its lifetime! It is little wonder that people are so afraid of sharks. We often hear stories from Australia of shark attacks where legs get bitten off or people are killed by sharks. The film *Jaws* didn't help us feel any better about sharks because it was all about a dangerous, big shark that was killing people. Even though the shark used in that exciting film wasn't real, people became more afraid of sharks. Usually, sharks eat alone. Like whales, sharks eat huge amounts of plankton. Sometimes, when one shark is feeding it attracts others. They swim up as quickly as possible and all begin to try to get a piece of the meal. They bite anything that gets in their way – even each other. Sharks live on a diet of fish and mammals (like seals) and have even been known to eat seagulls[3]. Sharks will sometimes eat other sharks. For example, a tiger shark might eat a bull shark! Their teeth are sharp and pointy. Some are quite harmless. Oddly enough, the least dangerous sharks tend to be the largest! On average, there are only about 100 shark attacks each year and only 10 of those result in a human death. People, however, kill thousands of sharks a year for sport and for food. Shark skins are used to make products like any other leather would be. Shark soup and shark steaks are both eaten in countries such as the United States and Australia.

Annotations
1 *shark*: Hai
2 *jaw*: Kiefer
3 *seagull*: Möve

A True or false? (12 pts.)

Mark the correct statements and correct those that are wrong.

	true	false
1. Some whales have stronger jaws than a big shark has.	☐	☐
_______________		
2. Sharks are born and die in water.	☐	☐
_______________		
3. People are often badly injured by sharks.	☐	☐
_______________		
4. Sharks only eat plankton, seals and seagulls.	☐	☐
_______________		
5. People all over the world eat shark meat and soup.	☐	☐
_______________		
6. People are very frightened of sharks.	☐	☐
_______________		

B Summary (4 pts.)

Explain in English what effect the film *Jaws* had on the way people see sharks.

____

____

____

____

II Give synonyms (3 pts.)

1. very surprised _______________
2. very large _______________
3. (to) produce _______________

III Grammar (6 pts.)

Adjective or adverb? Fill in the blanks with the right form of the word in brackets.

1. Many people visit Ireland _______________ (regular).
2. The weather there can sometimes be quite ___________ (rough).

3. In summer the sun in Ireland shines _______________ (bright).
4. The sky is often _______________ (blue).
5. There are clouds too and lots of showers. Anyone living there must ___________________ (sure) get wet twice a day.
6. The All-Ireland Hurling final __________________ (normal) takes place on the first Sunday in September.

IV Composition (20 pts.)

You work for a school magazine in Australia. There has been more and more shark activity in the area and you have been asked to write an article warning students about swimming in dangerous waters, about going out too deep and swimming alone. Write the article and tell everyone about the last shark attack you can remember. Your article should have at least 150 words.

Solution

I Reading comprehension

A True or false?

		true	false
1.	Some whales have stronger jaws than a big shark has. Sharks have the strongest jaws in the world.	☐	☒
2.	Sharks are born and die in water.	☒	☐
3.	People are often badly injured by sharks.	☒	☐
4.	Sharks only eat plankton, seals and seagulls. Sharks sometimes eat other sharks.	☐	☒
5.	People all over the world eat shark meat and soup. Only people in some countries such as Australia eat shark meat and soup.	☐	☒
6.	People are very frightened of sharks.	☒	☐

B Summary

Jaws was a film that a lot of people watched and it showed sharks as dangerous and frightening. The shark in the film was not a real shark but it went on killing people so that people in the cinemas became more and more afraid of sharks.

II Give synonyms

1. amazed
2. huge
3. (to) make

III Grammar

1. Many people visit Ireland **regularly**.
2. The weather there can sometimes be quite **rough**.
3. In summer the sun in Ireland shines **brightly**.
4. The sky is often **blue**.
5. There are clouds too and lots of showers. Anyone living there must **surely** get wet twice a day.
6. The All-Ireland Hurling final **normally** takes place on the first Sunday in September.

IV Composition

Hinweis: *Du bekommst hier 8 Punkte für den Inhalt, wenn dein Text alle verlangten Informationen enthält und wenn du einen informativen Zeitungsartikel verfasst hast. Für jede vergessene Information musst du dir einen Punkt abziehen. Ebenso musst du dir einen Punkt abziehen, wenn du nicht an Form und Stil eines Zeitungsartikels gedacht hast. Denke außerdem daran, dir für die sprachlichen Fehler Punkte abzuziehen.*

Shark attacks: Reducing the risk

The first thing to remember is that shark attacks don't happen very often. Most attacks happen near the shore. It is important to follow a number of rules when going to the beach so as to keep the risk of an attack low. I have put together a few basic rules for all of you to follow. They include:

- Always stay in groups as sharks often attack a person who is on his or her own.
- Do not wander too far from the shore – you are far from help if you need it.
- Don't go into the water in the darkness.
- Do not enter the water if you are bleeding from an open wound. Sharks smell blood.
- Don't wear shiny jewelry because the light makes a shark think you are a fish.
- Don't go into dirty waters or places where sharks are known to feed.
- Don't allow your pet into the water.
- Do not enter the water if sharks are known to be present and leave the water if sharks are seen while there.

The last time we had a shark attack in our area the girl who was injured went swimming alone and took her dog with her. She was also wearing rings on her finger and we think this made the shark think she was a fish. She lost three fingers and suffered bad leg injuries before she managed to get out of the water. Please be careful. Sharks are part of our world and we have to be sensible when we go swimming.

Notenschlüssel:

1	2	3	4	5	6
45–40	39–34	33–29	28–23	22–17	16–0

Klassenarbeit 4
Schwerpunkte: ***Listening comprehension, mediation, grammar, composition***

45 minutes

I Listening comprehension (12 pts.)

Peter and his sister Anne are visiting their Aunt Mary in Dublin. They are making plans for the day.

True or false?

Are these statements true or false? If they are false explain why. (true / false)

1. Both children know which bus to take to get into town. ☐ ☐

   ____

2. They are to get off the bus at Trinity College. ☐ ☐

   ____

3. Anne needs a new handbag and some new shoes. ☐ ☐

   ____

4. Peter just wants to go to see the Book of Kells and to visit the Guinness museum. ☐ ☐

   ____

5. Anne thinks they shouldn't stay together for all the time in Dublin. ☐ ☐

   ____

6. It's difficult to get to the Irish Writers Museum. ☐ ☐

   ____

7. You have to have the exact sum of money needed on Dublin buses. ☐ ☐

   ____

8. The children decide to take a packed lunch. ☐ ☐

   ____

II Mediation (10 pts.)

You are Anne and you go to visit Virgin Records. While you are there you hear a German woman trying to find out the price of a CD. She has however very poor English and the Irish person has no German. Help them understand each other.

ANNE: ____

MAN AT THE COUNTER: Oh that would be great. I can't understand a word the woman is saying.

ANNE: ____

WOMAN: Wie nett. Ich wollte fragen wie viel diese CD kostet.

ANNE: ____

MAN: Oh so that's what she wanted. It costs 14 euro.

ANNE: ____

WOMAN: Oh, das ist teuer. Das überlege ich mir noch.

ANNE: ____

MAN: That's fine, there are more CDs like this one on the left-hand side of the shop.

ANNE: ____

WOMAN: Vielen Dank. Und danken Sie bitte dem jungen Mann.

ANNE: ____

III Turn into the passive voice (8 pts.)

1. We feed our cat at 7 o'clock.

   ____

2. My father allowed Peter to go out every Saturday night last year.

   ____

3. All students would have passed the test if it had been easier.

   ____

4. Many Londoners visit Europe during the summer.

   ____

IV Give definitions (6 pts.)

1. souvenir

   ____

2. century

   ____

3. reliable

   ____

V Composition (22 pts.)

Imagine you are Peter or Anne. It is the day after your trip to the city centre. Write a letter to your mother telling what you did the day before. Use the information from the listening comprehension, the mediation and these photos to give you ideas. Write about 200 words.

Solution

I Listening comprehension

Hinweis: *Du kannst dir den Text zwei Mal anhören. Versuche beim ersten Hören, den groben Inhalt des Textes zu verstehen. Beim zweiten Hören konzentrierst du dich auf die Textstellen, die zur Beantwortung der Fragen nötig sind. Schwierige Vokabeln in diesem Text sind „traffic report", „fare", „to split up".*

A visit to Ireland

Peter and his sister Anne are visiting their Aunt Mary in Dublin. It is a lovely summer's day but unfortunately Aunt Mary has to work so they are making plans for the day until she is home again.

PETER: What will we do today?

ANNE: Well I've just heard the traffic report. There's a traffic jam just two miles down the Belfast Road so we'd better go towards the city centre!

PETER: Don't worry Anne. It could be much worse. There's plenty to do in Dublin. We could catch a bus into town and go from place to place.

ANNE: If only we knew what bus to take!

PETER: Aunt Mary said we should take the 15A and get off at Trinity College.

ANNE: Great! Is that near the shops?

PETER: Let me check the map. Wait a minute! Yes it is.

ANNE: Super! I really need a new handbag and some socks.

PETER: I hope that won't take all day. Didn't we want to go to see the Book of Kells and visit the Guinness museum?

ANNE: I suppose so.

PETER: But we are sure to find some lovely souvenirs which we can buy for Mum and Dad.

ANNE: Okay.

PETER: But I want to go the Viking centre as well. It's just nearby.

ANNE: That sounds really boring. I think we should split up at some stage. I'd like to go to Virgin Records if I have the time. Do you know where that is?

PETER: Yes, it's on the road by the river. We should be able to find it quite easily.

ANNE: Do you want to go the Irish Writers museum as well as all the other places?

PETER: Well it's up at the top of O'Connell Street so we'd have to get a second bus there. It's not that easy to do. Perhaps we should do that on Saturday. Maybe Aunt Mary would take us in the car.

ANNE: Good idea.

PETER: Talking of transport, we mustn't forget to take a lot of small coins with us. Aunt Mary said you have to have the exact fare because they don't give you any change.

ANNE: Do you think we need a packed lunch?

PETER: It would be nice but I think we should get going. I'll treat you to lunch when we get into town.

ANNE: How nice of you! You must want something from me! What is it?

True or false?

		true	false
1.	Both children know which bus to take to get into town. Only Peter knows which bus to take because Aunt Mary told him so.	☐	☒
2.	They are to get off the bus at Trinity College.	☒	☐
3.	Anne needs a new handbag and some new shoes. She needs a handbag and new socks.	☐	☒
4.	Peter just wants to go to see the Book of Kells and to visit the Guinness museum. Peter also wants to go to the Viking Centre.	☐	☒
5.	Anne thinks they shouldn't stay together for all the time in Dublin.	☒	☐
6.	It's difficult to get to the Irish Writers Museum.	☒	☐
7.	You have to have the exact sum of money needed on Dublin buses.	☒	☐
8.	The children decide to take a packed lunch. Peter offers Anne to buy lunch.	☐	☒

II Mediation

ANNE: **Excuse me, can I help? I speak a little German.**

MAN AT THE COUNTER: Oh that would be great. I can't understand a word the woman is saying.

ANNE: **Kann ich Ihnen helfen?**

WOMAN: Wie nett. Ich wollte fragen, wie viel diese CD kostet.

ANNE: **The lady wants to know how much the CD costs.**

MAN: Oh so that's what she wanted. It costs 14 euro.

ANNE: **Sie kostet 14 Euro. Möchten Sie sie kaufen?**

WOMAN: Oh, das ist teuer. Das überlege ich mir noch.

ANNE: **She thinks that's expensive. She would like to think about it.**

MAN: That's fine, there are more CDs like this one on the left-hand side of the shop.

ANNE: **Kein Problem. Es gibt noch weitere CDs dieser Art auf der linken Seite des Ladens.**

WOMAN: Vielen Dank. Und danken Sie bitte dem jungen Mann.

ANNE: **The lady says thanks very much. Bye-bye.**

III Turn into the passive voice

1. Our cat is fed at 7 o'clock.
2. Peter was allowed by my father to go out every Saturday night last year.
3. The test would have been passed by all students if it had been easier.
4. Europe is visited by many Londoners during the summer.

IV Give definitions

1. A souvenir is something you bring back from your holiday so that you remember your time there.
2. One hundred years are one century. We live in the 21st century.
3. A person who is reliable does what he says he will do.

V Composition

Hinweis: *Überlege dir, was in deinem Brief stehen soll. Denke daran, auch die Bilder in deinen Bericht an deine Mutter mit einzuarbeiten. Die maximale Punktzahl für den Inhalt sind 8 Punkte. Ziehe wieder für jede vergessene Information einen Punkt ab. Ebenso musst du dir Punkte abziehen, wenn du die Bilder nicht in deinen Bericht integriert hast und wenn du nicht die angemessene Anrede und Verabschiedung gewählt hast.*

Dear Mum,
How are you all? Peter and I arrived safely and are really enjoying the beautiful weather. Yesterday Aunt Mary had to work so we went into the city centre. She told us what bus to take and we got out at Trinity College. We went in see the famous Book of Kells. It was fantastic. Later we went on to the Guinness factory and I picked up some presents for both you and Dad. In the afternoon we went on a bus tour and saw a lot of the city and then I went to Virgin Records

and bought a folk album. While I was there a lady from Germany who spoke no English needed help so I tried out my German. Miss Blair would have been proud of me! Peter took me for lunch and we had a lovely snack in a famous Irish pub: Mulligan's.

The only thing I didn't like was the bus ride home. The bus was full of people, the driver wasn't friendly at all, and Peter nearly got thrown off the bus for having no change. Taking a bus is much nicer in London. I have to go now as we are going with Aunt Mary to the seaside for a walk. My feet are still killing me after yesterday but I can't say no.

Lots of love

Anne

Notenschlüssel:

1	2	3	4	5	6
58–50	49–41	40–34	33–28	27–20	19–0

Klassenarbeit 5
Schwerpunkte: ***Reading comprehension, mediation, vocabulary, composition***

45 minutes

I Reading comprehension

Scotland is famous for its beautiful landscape, great music and whisky. Other parts of Scottish life that most people have heard of include the Scottish kilt, Nessie the Loch Ness Monster and the Highland Games. The Highland Games, as you may know, take place in Scotland each summer. The Games are a series of traditional sporting events in different parts of the country where people come to watch athletes from Scotland and other parts of the world take part in many traditional Scottish sports. Colourful, competitive and exciting are three words people often think of when talking about the Games. Even the Queen often comes to the Braemar Games, the biggest Highland Games of them all. So what do we know of the history of the Games? The Highland Games have been held in Scotland for over 1,000 years and simple traditional Games testing speed[1] and strength[2] were held in the Highlands of Scotland in very early times. In 1848 the Highland Games were visited by Queen Victoria. Afterwards they became very popular. By this time the competitions were very like they are today. They included hammer throwing, tossing the caber[3], piping[4] and dancing along with running and jumping events. What a lot of people do not know is the fact that Highland Games take place not only in Scotland but also everywhere Scottish people went. This is true of the island of Nova Scotia, a part of Canada. The name Nova Scotia means New Scotland and many Scottish people settled there in the 18th, 19th and 20th centuries. Today you can find people living there who have very common Scottish names like MacPhail, McIntosh or Douglas. The area in Nova Scotia known as Antigonish is a good example. The Antigonish Highland Games first took place on October 16th, 1863. Events included foot races, piping, and traditional Scottish sports such as throwing the hammer. Five years later there were more different kinds of competitions so that people could take part in dancing, singing and fighting competitions. At the time only men were allowed to take part in the Games. As many as three thousand people would come together in the small town of Antigonish to enjoy the festival at this time. When World War I began, however, the Games were stopped but they soon started again after it ended. Since 1919, the Antigonish Highland Games have grown bigger and bigger. Often used to raise money for poor families in the area the Games now also see a number of musical concerts take place in the month of August. The Games have over the years helped the people of Nova Scotia remember and celebrate their Scottish roots[5] and keep the link to Scotland strong.

Annotations
1 *speed*: Schnelligkeit
2 *strength*: Stärke
3 *tossing the caber*: Baumstammüberschlag
4 *piping*: Dudelsackspielen
5 *root*: Wurzel

Questions on the text (12 pts.)

1. Why are the Highland Games so important a part of Scottish life?

   ____

   ____

2. Explain how the Games became so important.

   ____

   ____

3. Why can you say that Nova Scotia is quite Scottish?

   ____

   ____

4. What effect did World War I have on the Games in Nova Scotia?

   ____

   ____

5. What good things do people in Nova Scotia get from the Highland Games?

   ____

   ____

6. What competitions would you find at the Highland Games?

   ____

   ____

II Mediation (12 pts.)

In your English lesson you read the text about the Highland Games. You are fascinated and tell your family about this. Try to persuade them to go to Scotland or Canada in your holidays to visit the Games. Write about 100 words in German.

III Give the opposite (6 pts.)

1. exciting ____________________
2. (to) push ____________________
3. different ____________________

IV Composition: A postcard from Edinburgh (18 pts.)

For many years your parents have wanted to go to Scotland on a holiday. Now you are in Edinburgh and you are writing a postcard to your parents. Use the photos for ideas. Describe what you have seen so far. Write at least 200 words.

Solution

I Reading comprehension

Questions on the text

1. The Games are important because they give athletes a chance to take part in Scottish sports and people come from all around to watch them. Even the Queen sometimes visits. They are a traditional part of Scottish life.
2. Although the Games have existed for many centuries it was in the 19th century that they became really important. In 1848 even Queen Victoria took an interest. Soon the Games became very popular and they grew in importance.
3. First of all the name of the place itself is Scottish – it means new Scotland. There are many families in the area who have Scottish names and the people play Scottish sports as well. There are Highland Games in Nova Scotia and they are used to keep the link with Scotland alive. This shows that Nova Scotia is quite Scottish.
4. The effect was not a good one. When the war broke out the Games had to be stopped because the men were fighting and could not take part in them. After the war the Games started again.
5. Money is raised to help poor families and people can enjoy the concerts that are held around the same time. The Games help people understand their history and traditions and keep the link to Scotland alive.
6. There are many different sports such as throwing the hammer or piping. There are also dancing, singing and fighting competitions.

II Mediation

Heute haben wir im Englischunterricht einen Text über die schottischen Highland Games gelesen. Ich dachte immer, Schottland sei langweilig, aber diese Wettkämpfe klingen interessant. Ich würde gerne einmal beim Hammerweitwurf oder beim Baumstammüberschlag zuschauen. Euch würden sicher auch die Wettkämpfe im Dudelsackspielen gefallen. Highland Games gibt es schon seit mehr als 1000 Jahren. Nachdem Queen Victoria sie einmal besuchte, wurden sie immer bekannter und beliebter. Könnten wir nicht in den nächsten Sommerferien zu den Highland Games nach Braemar fahren? Dort sehen wir vielleicht sogar die Queen! Aber Highland Games gibt es nicht nur in Schottland. Falls euch Kanada besser gefällt, könnten wir auch dort Highland Games besuchen. Denn die schottischen Einwanderer in Antigonish haben ihre Tradition nach Kanada mitgebracht.

III Give the opposite

1. boring
2. (to) pull
3. similar

IV Composition: A postcard from Edinburgh

Hinweis: *Maximal kannst du hier 6 Punkte für den Inhalt bekommen. Dazu musst du über deine Reise in Schottland berichtet, entsprechende Sehenswürdigkeiten erwähnt, die richtige Briefform und die korrekte Begrüßung und Verabschiedung gewählt haben.*

Dear Mum and Dad, July 10th

Just a quick note from sunny Edinburgh. We are having a great time in Scotland. I have seen loads of beautiful castles and we seem to meet sheep everywhere. We were by the seaside and even saw sheep on the beach! Today we went for a walk in Edinburgh city centre. I bought new clothes and we met a Scottish bagpiper wearing a funny skirt they call a kilt. He was playing at the side of the road and loads of children stopped to listen to him. Although it wasn't my kind of music I gave him 2 euro. Last night we were in a pub called Ben Nevis. The sign outside had the words 'disco' and 'great value for money' written on it so we went in. I think Ben Nevis is the name of a mountain. We listened to music and had a great time. Tomorrow we head for Glasgow.

See you soon!

Jenny

Notenschlüssel:

1	2	3	4	5	6
48–43	42–37	36–31	30–25	24–17	16–0

Klassenarbeit 6

Schwerpunkte: ***Listening comprehension, vocabulary, grammar, mediation***

45 minutes

I Listening comprehension

Jack Green, a student at a Florida High School also works for the school magazine. Today he is interviewing Julie Landy, a NASA worker.

A True or false? (12 pts.)

Read these statements and say if they are true or false.
If they are false then you must explain why. — true false

1. Jack Green works for the school radio station. ☐ ☐

   ____

2. Julie Landy has worked for 20 years on the shuttle programme. ☐ ☐

   ____

3. Julie Landy is an astronaut. ☐ ☐

   ____

4. Julie Landy was not at work the day the Challenger shuttle exploded. ☐ ☐

   ____

5. According to what Julie says the shuttle has not been in space since 2003. ☐ ☐

   ____

6. NASA wants to make the shuttle safer. ☐ ☐

   ____

7. Julie likes working for NASA because the money she earns is very good. ☐ ☐

   ____

8. A shuttle mission usually takes about a week. ☐ ☐

   ____

B Statements (5 pts.)

Place the following statements in the correct order 1–5 as they appear in the text. Write the correct number next to the statement.

__ I work closely with our boss Mr Griffin.

__ You're welcome.

__ The shuttle has taken astronauts on many successful missions.

__ The future of the space shuttle programme depends on the success of the Discovery's journey.

__ How long does a shuttle mission usually last?

C Summary (3 pts.)

Summarise the information you get in the text concerning Miss Landy in English.

II Words and grammar

A Wordfield "space" (4 pts.)

All these words or phrases have to do with space and the space programme. Fill in the correct words.

1. A person who goes into space: __ __ __ R __ __ __ __ __
2. A word used to describe a group of people who work in a shuttle or plane: __ __ __ __
3. To mend something that is damaged: to __ __ __ __ __ __
4. "We __ __ __ __ L __ __ __ O __ __." These words are used when a shuttle is launched.

B If-clauses (6 pts.)

Fill in the correct form of the words in brackets.

1. If you ________________ (to drink) too much milk you ________________ (to get) ill.
2. John, you ________________ (to improve) your French if you ________________ (to work) harder.
3. It might snow tomorrow. If it ________________ (to snow) we ________________ (not, to play) tennis.

III Mediation

(20 pts.)

On a visit to the Kennedy Space Center with your father you meet a woman from Indiana called Tammy. Together you are waiting for the launch of the Discovery space shuttle. The weather however is not very good. Your father speaks very little English, Tammy speaks only a few words of German. Help Tammy and your father talk to one another.

FATHER: Was hat der Sprecher jetzt gesagt? Frag sie mal!

YOU: ____

TAMMY: Of course I can. He said the start has just been delayed by another 30 minutes.

YOU: ____

FATHER: Oh wie schade! Wissen Sie wieso?

YOU: ____

TAMMY. Yes. It's because of the bad weather off the coast.

YOU: ____

FATHER: Frag die Frau ob Sie schon eimmal hier war und wie das Wetter damals war.

YOU: ____

TAMMY: Yes, I was. I was here with my son Landon five years ago and we had brilliant weather. We saw the Columbia take off and it was very exciting.

YOU: ____

TAMMY: Would you like to go for a walk in the main building? You can see some old space shuttles from there. And there's a restaurant!

YOU: ____

FATHER: Das wäre großartig! Aber nur wenn wir Sie zu eine Tasse Kaffee einladen dürfen.

TAMMY: Now that's an offer I couldn't refuse. But we have to be back in twenty minutes so let's hurry.

YOU: ____

Solution

I Listening comprehension

***Hinweis:** Die schwierigen Vokabeln hier sind: „scientific gains“, „damaged“.*

Interview with a NASA worker

Jack Green, a student at a Florida High School also works for the school magazine. Today he is interviewing Julie Landy, a NASA worker who has 20 years experience of working on the space shuttle programme. Jack has been sitting waiting for Miss Landy for a while because she had a meeting but now they can talk.

JACK: Miss Landy, can you tell me something about your work with the space shuttle?

MISS LANDY: Certainly, Jack. The space shuttle programme is 25 years old and it has had highs and lows in that time. I started working here as a young science graduate just out of university. I'm an engineer and I work closely with our boss Mr Griffin and the rest of his team. I find it very exciting work even if you do get very tired and very worried at times. The best thing about my work here is that I am doing a job I always wanted to do ever since I saw the landing on the moon on TV as a young girl.

JACK: How long does a shuttle mission usually last?

MISS LANDY: I would say about 7 or 8 days.

JACK: So what have been the highlights in your time here?

MISS LANDY: Well, the shuttle has taken astronauts on many successful missions, resulting in super scientific gains for us all. The amount of information we have collected is of great use to the whole world and has helped scientists in all areas of work.

JACK: And the low points?

MISS LANDY: That would have to be the Challenger explosion in 1986. I was sitting at my desk when I saw it happen on the screen in front of me. I was only three weeks on the job and it was terrible to see grown men and women crying all around me and not being able to help. Then in 2003 the Columbia space shuttle broke up on re-entry over Texas.

JACK: So what has been done since then to make the shuttle safer?

MISS LANDY: Well as you know, the shuttles have been grounded since 2003. We are working on their design to improve their safety. It's not easy however. In 2005 the shuttle Discovery lost a large piece of its tank and we all had to begin again.

JACK: Is it the time to end the shuttle programme?

MISS LANDY: The future of the space shuttle programme depends on the success of the Discovery's journey. If all goes well NASA plans two more flights but if the shuttle is damaged at launch for example then my boss Michael Griffin has said that he would shut the programme down. And, Jack, if the programme shuts down, the next trip to space may not take place for another five years.

JACK: Thank you for your time and the information you have given us.

MISS LANDY: You're welcome.

A True or false?

		true	false
1.	Jack Green works for the school radio station. He works for the school magazine.	☐	☒
2.	Julie Landy has worked for 20 years on the shuttle programme.	☒	☐
3.	Julie Landy is an astronaut. She works for the shuttle programme but not as an astronaut.	☐	☒
4.	Julie Landy was not at work the day the Challenger shuttle exploded. She was sitting at her desk.	☐	☒
5.	According to what Julie says the shuttle has not been in space since 2003.	☒	☐
6.	NASA wants to make the shuttle safer.	☒	☐
7.	Julie likes working for NASA because the money she earns is very good. She likes doing a job that she always wanted to do.	☐	☒
8.	A shuttle mission usually takes about a week.	☒	☐

B Statements

(1) I work closely with our boss Mr Griffin.

(5) You're welcome.

(3) The shuttle has taken astronauts on many successful missions.

(4) The future of the space shuttle programme depends on the success of the Discovery's journey.

(2) How long does a shuttle mission usually last?

C Summary

Miss Landy is a highly-qualified, expert and hard-working member of the shuttle team. She is not an astronaut but is still very important. She studied science before starting work on the shuttle programme. She is friendly and well-spoken but she is also very busy.

II Words and grammar

A Wordfield "space"

1. astronaut
2. crew
3. repair
4. have lift off

B If-clauses

1. If you **drink** too much milk you **will get** ill.
2. John, you **would improve** your French if you **worked** harder.
3. It might snow tomorrow. If it **snows** we **won't play** tennis.

III Mediation

FATHER: Was hat der Sprecher jetzt gesagt? Frag sie mal!

YOU: **Excuse me, can you tell me what the person has just said?**

TAMMY: Of course I can. He said the start has just been delayed by another 30 minutes.

YOU: **Selbstverständlich. Der Start verzögert sich noch einmal um 30 Minuten.**

FATHER: Oh wie schade! Wissen Sie wieso?

YOU: **That's a pity. Do you know why?**

TAMMY. Yes. It's because of the bad weather off the coast.

YOU: **Ja, es liegt am schlechtem Wetter vor der Küste.**

FATHER: Frag die Frau ob Sie schon einmal hier war und wie das Wetter damals war.

YOU: **My father would like to know if you have been here before and what the weather was like then?**

TAMMY: Yes, I was. I was here with my son Landon five years ago and we had brilliant weather. We saw the Columbia take off and it was very exciting.

YOU: **Sie war vor fünf Jahren zusammen mit ihrem Sohn hier. Damals war das Wetter sehr schön. Sie sah den Start der Columbia und es war sehr spannend.**

TAMMY: Would you like to go for a walk in the main building? You can see some old space shuttles from there. And there's a restaurant!

YOU: **Sie fragt, ob wir Lust auf einem Spaziergang im Hauptgebäude haben. Man kann einige alte Raumfähren von dort aus sehen. Und dort gibt es auch ein Restaurant.**

FATHER: Das wäre großartig! Aber nur wenn wir Sie zu eine Tasse Kaffee einladen dürfen.

YOU: **That would be great. But only if you allow us to buy you a cup of coffee.**

TAMMY: Now that's an offer I couldn't refuse. But we have to be back in twenty minutes so let's hurry.

YOU: **Dieses Angebot kann sie nicht ablehnen. Aber wir müssen in 20 Minuten wieder da sein. Wir sollten uns also beeilen.**

Notenschlüssel:

1	2	3	4	5	6
50–45	44–39	38–32	31–26	25–18	17–0

Klassenarbeit 7
Schwerpunkte: *Reading comprehension, grammar, composition*

I Reading comprehension

The Battle of Hastings

October the 14th 1066, is a famous date in British history. It was on that day that England's most famous battle, the Battle of Hastings, took place. It was a battle between the French leader, William of Normandy, who is now often called William the Conqueror, and the Saxon King, Harold II of Britain. Between them they had about 15,000 men. William and his men had been preparing the invasion of England since early spring of the same year. He was a general with a lot of experience and had fought many battles. In late September William sailed for England and landed his army of soldiers at Pevensay in Sussex. Harold's army of men, who were not as well trained as William's moved towards Hastings to stop the invaders. Harold, however, had other problems on his mind as he got ready to make war. Firstly, he had just heard that the Pope had decided against Harold and wanted to ban him from the church. Even worse was the fact that Harold's own brother was causing him trouble in the north where he had joined with a Viking king to take power from Harold. The battle began early in the morning with William and his men fighting from the bottom of a hill. Harold made the mistake of putting his soldiers too closely together so that many of his men died. Even though William, too, saw a lot of his men killed in the battle he was able to make the Englishmen move out of position. He got them to chase him because he acted as if he wanted to run away. William then told his men to suddenly turn around and rush back into battle. The English were not ready for this surprise and many of their leading soldiers, even two of the king's brothers, were killed. When King Harold himself died late in the afternoon his soldiers still fought on for a while. As night fell, however, they began to leave the battlefield and by the next morning all had left and the success of William's clever move was there for everyone to see. Afterwards William moved his men towards London and he became King William I on December 25th. With the arrival of the Normans a new English culture was born. The Normans started building castles all over the country. In the beginning, most of these were of wood but later they were built of stone. Although William was now King of England, he was also Duke of Normandy and this made England a very important European power.

A True, false or not in the text? (9 pts.)

Select the right answer.

	true	false	not in text
1. The Battle of Hastings was the most famous battle in English history.	☐	☐	☐
2. About 5,000 men fought that day.	☐	☐	☐
3. Harold's army was the invading army.	☐	☐	☐
4. Harold had the good idea to place his soldiers closely together.	☐	☐	☐
5. Harold was a good and well-liked king.	☐	☐	☐
6. The Normans built only wooden castles in England.	☐	☐	☐

B Mediation (5 pts.)

Your history teacher heard that you were talking about the Battle of Hastings in your English lesson. He wants to know what problems Harold had when he went into battle. He asks you to sum up the most important aspects in German. Write 50–60 words.

II Vocabulary (3 pts.)

Think of words with a similar meaning for the underlined words.

1. William was <u>a general</u> with a lot of experience.

   ____

2. The Saxons weren't <u>afraid</u> of the Normans.

   ____

3. William and <u>all his soldiers</u> were positioned at the bottom of a hill.

   ____

III Grammar (14 pts.)

Fill in the right word or form of the word in brackets.

Last Sunday John Mills __________________ (to spend) three hours _______________ (for/at/by) the Notting Hill Carnival. The Carnival __________________________ (to take place) during the last weekend in August every year. It is one of the most famous festivals you will find anywhere in the world. Miss Walsh, John's favourite teacher, _________ (to be) also there. "Hello, John", she _________________ (to cry) from across the road. "Hi, Miss Walsh", John ____________ (to reply) and waved back to her. "I ____________________________ (to wait) here for my husband ___________ (since or for) 12 o'clock. You haven't seen him, have you?" she asked. John ______________ (to shake) his head and ____________________ (to go) off to buy an ice-cream. There were hundreds of people in beautiful costumes and John _____________________ (to watch) the parades go by. He ____________ (to think) it was really exciting. John _____________ (to hear) one policeman say to another "I'm going home soon. I hope my wife ____________________ (to prepare) a nice Sunday meal for me by now. I'm really hungry".

IV Composition (18 pts.)

Your local newspaper wants a report on a visit to the scene of the Battle of Hastings. You should describe the day you visited Hastings from school. Write about 200 words.

Solution

I Reading comprehension

A True, false or not in the text?

	true	false	not in text
1. The Battle of Hastings was the most famous battle in English history.	✗		
2. About 5,000 men fought that day.		✗	
3. Harold's army was the invading army.		✗	
4. Harold had the good idea to place his soldiers closely together.	✗		
5. Harold was a good and well-liked king.			✗
6. The Normans built only wooden castles in England.		✗	

B Mediation

Als Harold in die Schlacht bei Hastings zog hatte er viele unterschiedliche Probleme. Zum einen waren die Soldaten von Wilhelm dem Eroberer viel besser ausgebildet als die von Harold. Ein weiteres Problem war, dass der Papst Harold drohte, ihn aus der Kirche auszuschließen. Außerdem bereitete ihm auch sein Bruder Probleme. Denn dieser hatte sich mit einem Wikinger-König zusammengeschlossen und kämpfte nun gegen Harold.

II Vocabulary

1. William was **a leader** with a lot of experience.
2. The Saxons weren't **scared** of the Normans.
3. William and **his army** were positioned at the bottom of a hill.

III Grammar

Last Sunday John Mills **spent** three hours **at** the Notting Hill Carnival. The Carnival **takes place** during the last weekend in August every year. It is one of the most famous festivals you will find anywhere in the world. Miss Walsh, John's favourite teacher, **was** also there. “Hello, John”, she **cried** from across the road. “Hi, Miss Walsh”, John **replied** and waved back to her. “I **have been waiting** here for my husband **since** 12 o'clock. You haven't seen him, have you?” she asked. John **shook** his head and **went** off to buy an ice-cream. There were hundreds of people in beautiful costumes and John **watched** the parades go by. He **thought** it was really exciting. John **heared** one policeman say to another “I'm going home soon. I hope my wife **has prepared** a nice Sunday meal for me by now. I'm really hungry”.

IV Composition

***Hinweis:** Hier kannst du maximal 6 Punkte für den Inhalt und 12 Punkte für die Sprache bekommen.*

Our history teacher, Mr Mullins, took us to Hastings last week as part of our project on famous English battles. We all had to get up really early and travelled by bus from Bristol. We started off with a visit to a local museum where a friend of our teacher explained some of the political reasons why the battle took place and we saw a lot of interesting exhibitions. Then we had a short lunch before we were taken to the battle site itself. We could walk around and see exactly where the men fought and we travelled by bus from one place of historic importance to another. I took loads of photos and some of the girls did drawings. Unfortunately, it started to rain in the afternoon but Mr Mullins had arranged a short stop at a local abbey where we saw some documents that belonged to that time and a very nice guide told us some funny stories about things that are supposed to have happened during the battle. He told us all about King Harold's problems with the Pope in Rome and I thought that was the most interesting part. Finally, around 4.30 p.m. we went back to Bristol.

Notenschlüssel:

1	2	3	4	5	6
49–45	44–40	39–35	34–29	28–22	21–0

Klassenarbeit 8
Schwerpunkte: *Listening comprehension, grammar, composition*

I Listening comprehension (13 pts.)

Harriet Thompson is a guide at Liverpool Maritime Museum.
Listen to the information she gives about Liverpool and sea life.

True or false?

Say if the statement is true or false and if it is false say why. true false

1. Historians agree that less than 12 million people were sent to the other side of the world. ☐ ☐

____

____

2. The ships returned to Europe with things like sugar, coffee and tobacco. ☐ ☐

____

____

3. In the 18th and early 19th centuries some slaves *(= Sklaven)* in Britain started to fight other slaves. ☐ ☐

____

____

4. There is an International Slavery Museum just across the road from the Maritime Museum. ☐ ☐

____

____

5. Farm owners were not afraid of slaves. ☐ ☐

____

____

6. Slaves from the same families often saw each other again after getting to America. ☐ ☐

____

____

7. Liverpool was an important slave port and its ships were an important part of the Atlantic slave trade in the second half of the 18th century. ☐ ☐

____

____

8. The town and its people became very well-known because of the transport of slaves. ☐ ☐

____

____

II Grammar (7 pts.)

Join the following sentences using *relative pronouns*.

1. Liverpool is the name of a city in England.
   This photograph was taken there.

____

2. The man is wearing a cap. He bought it a year ago.

____

3. Who are the puppets? Their clothes are grey.

___

4. The machine plays music. The man works it by hand.

___

5. Tourists like to listen to the Beatles. They give money to the man.

___

6. The photographer saw the man. The man was sitting on a chair.

___

7. Beatles music is popular all over the world. It is played in pubs, on radio and at festivals.

___

III Vocabulary (6 pts.)

Explain the following words from the text.

1. slave ___

___

2. port ___

___

3. exhibition ___

___

IV Composition (14 pts.)

Imagine you are an officer on board a slave ship after it has just set sail from Liverpool and is half-way across the Atlantic. Write a diary entry about the first half of your trip to Carolina. Explain how you feel, what the weather is like, and how the slaves are on board the ship as well as anything else you can think of.

Solution

I Listening comprehension

Hinweis: Die schwierigen Vokabeln in diesem Text sind „exhibition", „merchant" und „rebel".

A visit to the Liverpool Maritime Museum

HARRIET: Well everybody, as you have seen there is a great deal to learn about Liverpool and sea life here at the museum. This exhibition on slavery is the last part of our tour of the museum. As you may know Liverpool was a major slave port and its ships and merchants were an important part of the Atlantic slave trade in the second half of the 18th century. The town and its people became very rich from the transport of slaves. This helped build the port into one of the biggest ports in Britain. From about 1500 to about 1865 millions of Africans were sold as slaves and taken across the Atlantic by Europeans and Americans to work on farms and plantations.

MAN: So do we know exactly how many Africans were sent across the Atlantic?

HARRIET: Historians don't agree on this. Some say a figure of about 12 million people were sent to the other side of the world. They have used shipping records to come to this figure. Other historians however think the number of slaves is far bigger, nearer to 20 million. Here we know that Liverpool ships carried about 1.5 million Africans across the Atlantic during the 5,000 journeys made, most of them going to the Caribbean. Around 300 voyages were made to North America – to places such as Carolina, Virginia and Maryland. The ships returned to Europe with goods such as sugar, cotton, coffee and tobacco. Liverpool became a rich city because of trading in slaves.

MAN: So how did the slave trade end?

HARRIET: That's an interesting question. In the 18th and early 19th centuries slaves began to fight back and some people in Britain started to fight for the rights of slaves. These people formed themselves into a movement and they helped bring the British slave trade to an end in 1807. However, Liverpool's links with slavery continued through cotton and other trades that needed slave labour for much of the 19th century.

MAN: Can you tell us anything about the slaves and their lives in America?

HARRIET: Yes, I can. When the slaves got to the Americas they were first of all washed and then had to put on oil. The oil was used to cover the damage the sea journey caused to their bodies. The ship captains then sold the slaves directly to men who were looking for workers for their farms. Families were broken up in this way and usually never saw each other again. We often think of slaves as people who work in the fields but slaves did all sorts of work. They worked in mines, in towns or as cooks in the kitchen. They were very badly treated and this was because the farm owners were always afraid the slaves would rebel against them. In law slaves had no rights at all. If you are interested in finding out more about slaves then I suggest you visit the International Slavery Museum just across the road. Thank you for your attention.

True or false?

		true	false
1.	Historians agree that less than 12 million people were sent to the other side of the world. Historians are not able to agree on how many slaves were sent to the other parts of the world because some say 12 million were sent and others say the figure was far higher.	☐	☒
2.	The ships returned to Europe with things like sugar, coffee and tobacco.	☒	☐
3.	In the 18th and early 19th centuries some slaves in Britain started to fight other slaves. People started to fight for the rights of slaves.	☐	☒
4.	There is an International Slavery Museum just across the road from the Maritime Museum.	☒	☐
5.	Farm owners were not afraid of slaves. The farm owners were afraid of slaves rebelling against them.	☐	☒
6.	Slaves from the same families often saw each other again after getting to America. They hardly ever saw each other again.	☐	☒
7.	Liverpool was an important slave port and its ships were an important part of the Atlantic slave trade in the second half of the 18th century.	☒	☐
8.	The town and its people became very well-known because of the transport of slaves. They became very rich from the transport of slaves.	☐	☒

II Grammar

Hinweis: *Wenn du bei den Relativsätzen unsicher sein solltest, kannst du die Regeln in der Kurzgrammatik S. 11–12 nachlesen.*

1. Liverpool is the name of a city in England where this photograph was taken.
2. The man is wearing a cap that/which he bought a year ago.

3. Who are the puppets whose clothes are grey?
4. The machine, which the man works by hand, plays music.
5. Tourists, who give money to the man, like to listen to the Beatles.
6. The photographer saw the man who was sitting on a chair.
7. Beatles music, which is played in pubs, on radio and at festivals, is popular all over the world.

III Vocabulary

1. Slaves were people who had to do very hard work but didn't get any money. They had no rights and had to follow the orders of their owner.
2. A port is the place where ships arrive or depart.
3. In the Liverpool Maritime Museum you can see an exhibition about sea life in Liverpool.

IV Composition

Hinweis: *Hier bekommst du 5 Punkte für den Inhalt, wenn dein Tagebucheintrag alle Informationen enthält, die in der Aufgabenstellung genannt sind.*

I have come to my cabin to get away from the terrible winds and waves that are beating our ship. We left Liverpool a week ago and sailed past the south-west coast of Ireland. The start of the trip went very well, sunshine and little rain. But since we have been out in the Atlantic things have got much worse. It has rained for three days and three nights. The ship moves from side to side and I don't know how the men on top can stand this. We lost one man overboard last Saturday and could not find him. He was a good sailor and a father of nine children. The captain says he has has never seen a storm as bad as this one. Last night I had to check on the slaves. I took two men with me when we went down in case they should make any trouble. I feel quite sorry for them because the food they get is terrible and the conditions below are horrible. We found one mother dead with her child crying beside her. I sometimes think that the people who say that what we are doing is inhuman are right. But I cannot say anything or I will lose my job. We gave the child to another woman who has said she will look after it. I must sleep now because I have had no rest in 48 hours. How I wish I had listened to my father and not joined this trip.

Notenschlüssel:

1	2	3	4	5	6
40–36	35–31	30–26	25–21	20–15	14–0

Klassenarbeit 9
Schwerpunkte: ***Grammar, translation, questions on selected topics***

45 minutes

I Words and grammar (14 pts.)

Put in the correct English word or phrase.

Jean suffered a very bad ________________ *(Verletzung)* on Bonfire Night last year when she ____________________ *(verletzen)* her arm while using a firework. The ________________________ *(Kranken-wagen)* was called and a ____________________ *(Sanitäter)* arrived after about ten minutes. The man had travelled by car and he ___________________ *(überholen)* a lot of cars on the way. Going around one corner he almost _____________________ *(zusammen-stoßen mit)* a woman on a bike who thought she was going _____________________ *(in die falsche Richtung)*. She had left the ________________ *(Radweg)* to _________________ *(überqueren)* to the other side of the road. She wasn't cycling ________________ *(vorsichtig)* enough! The poor woman ______________ *(bekommen)* a ___________________ *(schrecklich)* shock.

II Some, any or every? (6 pts.)

Fill in the correct form. Use *some, any, every* or one of their compound forms.

1. Are there ________________ books on the kitchen table, Mum?
2. I left ________________ books on it two hours ago.
3. Where has ____________________ gone to? The room was full a minute ago.
4. Is there ____________________ in the letter box? Have a look.
5. May I have __________________ sugar please?
6. My sister can't find her plate ____________________.

III Comparisons (4 pts.)

1. Mary is the ________________________ *(hübsch)* girl in the class.

2. New York is ________________________ *(groß)* Munich.

3. Tennis is ____________________________ *(aufregend)* squash,
   but football is the ____________________________ *(aufregend)*
   of the three sports.

IV Translation (28 pts.)

1. Peter flüsterte „Müssen wir wirklich jetzt ins Bett gehen?"
   „Natürlich! Es ist zwanzig nach acht", antwortete seine Mutter.

   ____

   ____

2. Braucht Vater noch etwas für das Mittagessen?

   ____

   ____

3. Die Kellnerin musste in die Küche gehen um den Kartoffelsalat
   zu holen.

   ____

   ____

4. Wir brauchten nicht zu helfen. Es waren viele Menschen dort.

   ____

   ____

V Questions on selected topics

1. Thanksgiving (6 pts.)

   A friend of yours has never heard of Thanksgiving. He would like to know when it happens, what the history of Thanksgiving is and what happens in America on Thanksgiving Day in homes and cities. Write down as much as you know.
   Write at least 60 words.

2. Write about 150 words on <u>one</u> of the following topics. (12 pts.)

a) Guy Fawkes and James Stuart

This is a drawing of Guy Fawkes being questioned by King James Stuart. Why did Guy Fawkes want to kill King James and how did he try to do it? How is Guy remembered today?

b) Shakespeare and the Globe Theatre

Describe a visit to the Globe Theatre in earlier times.

Solution

I Words and grammar

Jean suffered a very bad **injury** on Bonfire Night last year when she **hurt** her arm while using a firework. The **ambulance** was called and a **paramedic** arrived after about ten minutes. The man had travelled by car and he **had overtaken** a lot of cars on the way. Going around one corner he almost **crashed into** a woman on a bike who thought she was going **in the wrong direction**. She had left the **cycle lane** to **cross** to the other side of the road. She wasn't cycling **carefully** enough! The poor woman **got** a **terrible** shock.

II Some, any or every?

1. Are there **any** books on the kitchen table, Mum?
2. I left **some** books on it two hours ago.
3. Where has **everyone** gone to? The room was full a minute ago.
4. Is there **anything** in the letter box? Have a look.
5. May I have **some** sugar please?
6. My sister can't find her plate **anywhere**.

III Comparisons

1. Mary is the **most beautiful/prettiest** girl in the class.
2. New York is **bigger than** Munich.
3. Tennis is **as exciting as/more exciting than** squash, but football is the **most exciting** of the three sports.

IV Translation

1. Peter whispered: "Do we really have to go to bed now?" "Of course! It's twenty past eight," his mother answered.
2. Does Dad need anything for lunch?
3. The waitress had to go into the kitchen to fetch the potato salad.
4. We didn't have to help. There were lots of people.

V Questions on selected topics

1. Thanksgiving Day is an important national holiday in the USA. It is always celebrated on the fourth Thursday in November. On this day the whole family gathers. Often people travel all over the country to meet their relatives. Traditionally people have turkey for dinner on this special day. The custom goes back to the first settlers who came to America from Europe in search of freedom. They celebrated their first harvest and they also invited the Native Americans who had helped them get through their first winter.

2. a) In November 1605 Guy Fawkes together with several other Catholics planned to kill King James I. The king was a Protestant and under his reign Catholics were treated very badly. They had to practice their religion in secret. Therefore the Catholics wanted to get rid of James I. So they decided to blow up the English Parliament on the day when the king was going to open Parliament. However, this plan, known today as the Gunpowder Plot, didn't work out. Guy Fawkes was arrested and questioned by King James as you can see in this picture. Guy was hanged and English Protestants lit great bonfires every November 5th from that year on. Today this date is still known as Bonfire Night and people remember the historic event with fireworks. Many children also make models of Guy Fawkes. Around Bonfire Night they take their "guys" outside and ask for "a penny for the guy" in the streets. They use the money to buy fireworks and on the 5th of November they burn their "guys" on the bonfire they have built.

b) In Shakespeare's time the Globe was one of the most famous theatres in England. A visit to this theatre must have been a special experience. First of all you had to look whether the flag was up because this fact told you that there would be a performance. The Globe was a round building. But in contrast to modern theatres only the galleries had a roof. The rest of the theatre was an open air arena. Therefore the performances took place in the afternoon so that there was enough light. Only noblemen and other rich people could afford to sit in one of the galleries during the play. Ordinary people, called "groundlings", had to stand on the ground around the stage. For the groundlings, the play itself was often not the most important thing. During the performance they could buy food and drink, meet friends and talk about the latest news. What must have been fascinating is that you were very close to the actors because people stood directly in front of and around the stage. And – at least as a groundling – you could shout at the actors or even throw tomatoes if you didn't like the play. Another unusual thing is that the actors were all men; even female roles had to be played by men or boys.

Notenschlüssel:

1	2	3	4	5	6
70–61	60–52	51–43	42–34	33–25	24–0

(Bitte blättern Sie um)

Englisch Grundwissen

Englisch Grundwissen 5. Klasse .... Best.-Nr. 90505
Klassenarbeiten Englisch 5. Klasse mit CD ...... Best.-Nr. 905053
Englisch Grundwissen 6. Klasse .... Best.-Nr. 90506
Klassenarbeiten Englisch 6. Klasse mit CD ...... Best.-Nr. 905063
Englisch Grundwissen 7. Klasse .... Best.-Nr. 90507
Klassenarbeiten Englisch 7. Klasse mit CD ...... Best.-Nr. 905073
Englisch Grundwissen 8. Klasse .... Best.-Nr. 90508
Englisch Grundwissen 9. Klasse .... Best.-Nr. 90509
Englisch Grundwissen 10. Klasse .... Best.-Nr. 90510
Englisch Übertritt in die Oberstufe .... Best.-Nr. 82453

Englisch Kompakt-Wissen

Kompakt-Wissen Kurzgrammatik .... Best.-Nr. 90461
Kompakt-Wissen Grundwortschatz .... Best.-Nr. 90464

Englisch Textproduktion

Textproduktion 9./10. Klasse .... Best.-Nr. 90541

Englisch Leseverstehen

Leseverstehen 5. Klasse .... Best.-Nr. 90526
Leseverstehen 6. Klasse .... Best.-Nr. 90525
Leseverstehen 8. Klasse .... Best.-Nr. 90522
Leseverstehen 10. Klasse .... Best.-Nr. 90521

Englisch Hörverstehen

Hörverstehen 5. Klasse mit CD .... Best.-Nr. 90512
Hörverstehen 6. Klasse mit CD .... Best.-Nr. 90511
Hörverstehen 7. Klasse mit CD .... Best.-Nr. 90513
Hörverstehen 9. Klasse mit CD .... Best.-Nr. 90515
Hörverstehen 10. Klasse mit CD .... Best.-Nr. 80457

Englisch Rechtschreibung

Rechtschreibung und Diktat
5. Klasse mit 3 CDs .... Best.-Nr. 90531
Rechtschreibung und Diktat
6. Klasse mit 2 CDs .... Best.-Nr. 90532
Englische Rechtschreibung 9./10. Klasse .... Best.-Nr. 80453

Englisch Wortschatzübung

Wortschatzübung 5. Klasse mit CD .... Best.-Nr. 90518
Wortschatzübung 6. Klasse mit CD .... Best.-Nr. 90519
Wortschatzübung Mittelstufe .... Best.-Nr. 90520

Englisch Übersetzung

Translation Practice 1 / ab 9. Klasse .... Best.-Nr. 80451
Translation Practice 2 / ab 10. Klasse .... Best.-Nr. 80452

Englisch: Zentrale Prüfungen

Jahrgangsstufentest Englisch
6. Klasse mit CD Gymnasium Bayern .... Best.-Nr. 954661
Zentrale Klassenarbeit Englisch 10. Klasse mit CD
Gymnasium Baden-Württemberg.................. Best.-Nr. 80456
Vergleichsarbeiten Englisch
VERA 8. Klasse Gymnasium .... Best.-Nr. 954682
Zentrale Prüfung Englisch ZP 10 NRW .... Best.-Nr. 554601
Mittlerer Schulabschluss Berlin Englisch mit CD Best.-Nr. 111550
Mittlerer Schulabschluss/Sek I
Mündliche Prüfung Englisch Brandenburg ...... Best.-Nr. 121550
Besondere Leistungsfeststellung Englisch
10. Klasse mit CD Gymnasium Sachsen .... Best.-Nr. 1454601
Besondere Leistungsfeststellung Englisch
10. Klasse Gymnasium Thüringen .... Best.-Nr. 1654601

Französisch

Französisch im 1. Lernjahr .... Best.-Nr. 905502
Rechtschreibung und Diktat 1./2. Lernjahr
mit 2 CDs .... Best.-Nr. 905501
Französisch im 2. Lernjahr .... Best.-Nr. 905503
Französisch im 3. Lernjahr .... Best.-Nr. 905504
Französisch im 4. Lernjahr .... Best.-Nr. 905505
Wortschatzübung Mittelstufe .... Best.-Nr. 94510
Zentrale Klassenarbeit Französisch
10. Klasse Gymnasium Baden-Württemberg .. Best.-Nr. 80501
Kompakt-Wissen Kurzgrammatik .... Best.-Nr. 945011
Kompakt-Wissen Grundwortschatz .... Best.-Nr. 905001

Latein

Latein I/II im 1. Lernjahr 5./6. Klasse .... Best.-Nr. 906051
Latein I/II im 2. Lernjahr 6./7. Klasse .... Best.-Nr. 906061
Latein I/II im 3. Lernjahr 7./8. Klasse .... Best.-Nr. 906071
Übersetzung im 1. Lektürejahr .... Best.-Nr. 906091
Wiederholung Grammatik .... Best.-Nr. 94601
Wortkunde .... Best.-Nr. 94603
Kompakt-Wissen Kurzgrammatik .... Best.-Nr. 906011

Biologie/Chemie

Chemie – Mittelstufe 1 .... Best.-Nr. 90731
Besondere Leistungsfeststellung Biologie
10. Klasse Gymnasium Thüringen .... Best.-Nr. 1657001
Besondere Leistungsfeststellung Chemie
10. Klasse Gymnasium Thüringen .... Best.-Nr. 1657301

Geschichte

Kompakt-Wissen Geschichte
Unter-/Mittelstufe .... Best.-Nr. 907601

Ratgeber „Richtig Lernen"

Tipps und Lernstrategien – Unterstufe .... Best.-Nr. 10481
Tipps und Lernstrategien – Mittelstufe .... Best.-Nr. 10482